PARENTING COLLEGE FRESHMEN: CONSULTING FOR ADULTHOOD

By *[signature: Linda Bips]*

Linda L. Bips, Ed.D.

With

Jessica and Kristina Wallitsch

ISBN: 1-4107-2050-0 (e-book)
ISBN: 1-4107-2051-9 (Paperback)

This book is printed on acid free paper.

1stBooks – rev. 03/10/03

Acknowledgements

Thank you to my parents, Alma and Herman Bips, who first taught me the meaning of being a good parent and to my daughters, Jessica and Kristina, who taught me every day how to be the best parent I could be and to all the students over the years who continued my education and contributed their stories. Thank you to my colleagues, who supported and advised me, and who helped to make this book a reality.

Special thank you's to Shira Levin, my assistant who helped me get this book to print, and to Ilana Scharff, who read and edited the final manuscript.

WARNER BROS, PUBLICATIONS U.S. INC., Miami, FL 33014

PARENTING COLLEGE FRESHMEN:

CONSULTING FOR ADULTHOOD

Many times over the past seventeen years, parents of college students, friends, colleagues and my children have encouraged me to write this book. Numerous times I have answered the telephone in my counseling center office to hear a parent on the other end asking my recommendations. This book is my advice based on my experiences and my expertise on how to assist your college student before and during his first year.

I attended a small private liberal arts college from fall 1966 to May 1970. The times were intense and constantly changing. In our country there were assassinations and demands for equal rights for all. At our colleges, students demonstrated against the Vietnam war and social rules on campus. In this book, I will often refer to my college experiences as a point of comparison to today's college scene. We all try to understand the new by placing it in our frame of reference. Most of you will have attended college in the 60's and 70's. Remembering the way it was, really, not your idealized version, will allow you to empathize and understand the day-to-day ups and downs of your college student.

This book was germinating in my mind for many years and recently I realized that what would make this book unique and probably more usable are the voices of college students. My daughters, Jessica, class of 1998, and Kristina, class of 2002, have responded to my chapters on many of the topics in this book. Their purpose is to give you a student's view albeit influenced by having been raised by their college counselor mother.

Table of Contents

Chapter 1   Parenting - The Challenge of Fences

Fences

When I was a child, my guitar toting, cowboy-garbed Lithuanian uncle used to sing a cowpoke song, "Don't Fence Me In."

Give me land, lots of land under starry skies above
Don't fence me in.
Let me ride through the wide-open country that I love,
Don't fence me in
Let me be by myself in the evening breeze
Listen to the murmur of the cottonwood trees
Send me off forever but I ask you please
Don't fence me in.

I adopted this mantra for parenting my children before I sent them off to college. I often picture my long legged daughter as a colt. During her childhood, she was confined

1

to a small corral next to the barn under my sight and tutelage. As the days progressed, she was allowed out to pasture and to roam over larger and larger territories with outlying fences. I picture her running in the sunlight and tossing her head so her long hair flies in the wind - proud and sometimes defiant as she hurdles toward the fence - a boundary. The art of parenting is to know where to place the fences and when to move the fences out or in. You may call these fences rules like "Go to bed by 8:30pm," "Be home by midnight," or "Don't drink and drive." There always must be a fence or rule to identify the limits for the safety of the child. I have frequently watched my children use the fence in different ways. One of my daughters explored the pasture but frequently came back to the barn to check things out and to communicate. My other daughter would frequently trot rapidly along the edge of the fence at the very perimeter of my land, by hanging out at the mall or going to a local amusement park without an adult. Perhaps she was looking for broken rails so she could leap into the neighboring fields or even the free open range. She would often stay out in the field past my expectations. She even went off to boarding school for two years and wandered other fields with fences higher than mine. She immediately encountered structured study halls, restricted times for phone calls and even a lights out rule, which she circumvented with the aid of a miner's flashlight on her forehead, provided by her father. For a time she was willing to tolerate these restrictions in order to reach her goal - to be accepted by the best possible college. She was always happy to return to her home pastures. There she found room to run and fences farther from my home base, in other words less restrictive rules.

So what are the fences of good parenting? Rules, limits, expectations and boundaries are the essential fences. When your daughter goes to college, she leaves behind your fences. Your rules and regulations no longer are her daily limits. But how can we believe that she is capable and ready to run in the pastures beyond our neighborhoods?

Consulting on attaining adulthood

It is important at this time to make a major shift from a more traditional approach of parenting college students by facilitating separation to a more modern concept of consulting with them on attaining adulthood. You will want to draw on your own knowledge to assist your student in developing his/her intellectual, financial and interpersonal skills during the college years. Although you may want to become familiar with the college resources that are available to your student (see Appendix A – College Services), offer them such information only at their request. It is important to shift from arranging all the details or fixing every problem for your students to consulting with them and allowing them to effect their own outcomes and solve their own problems. Whether it is writing a paper for a course, mediating with a roommate or paying for parking tickets, it is critically important to your student's confidence and self worth that he acts on his own behalf. If you intervene and manage his life, you are not only inhibiting his development but also insulting him by letting him know that you don't think he can handle his own life. So before you pick up the phone or write that letter, stop and read this book.

Extended adolescence

Citizens of other countries often criticize higher education in the United States for prolonging adolescent dependency. This extended adolescence has become the reality in the psychological development of eighteen year olds. In the new century, the stages of late adolescence and young adulthood have been combined into the developmental stage of "emerging adulthood" and extended to the age of thirty (Arnett, 2000). Parents today want to be involved in the continuing development of their sons and daughters. The soccer moms and the little league fathers are unwilling to drop their children off at the college gates and relinquish their parenting roles to the college administrators and faculty. Many parents are even encouraging their sons and daughters to return home after graduating from college and resume an active role in the nuclear family. This was evident in a recent article in a national newsmagazine where a father explained that he really enjoyed having his twenty-year-old son living at home and playing golf together on Saturdays. A few years ago some referred to these 20 something's as boomerangs who, after college graduation, return to their parents' home and financial support and to the comforts of their parents' lifestyle. Even if your graduate is employed, he expects to spend freely and maybe bank some of his earnings for his future rather than pay rent today.

The four years of extended adolescence spent at college allow your student to experiment in a relatively safe environment. She may question her values concerning her political views, her attendance at your choice of religious institution, her sexual views and behaviors, her use of drugs and/or alcohol, and especially her choice of future occupation and lifestyle. Experimentation is the purpose of college. Freedom from parents allows the student to question and to be exposed to values that are different from her upbringing perhaps for the first time.

College student development

College student development has several theoretical bases. Erik Erikson (1963, 1968) was one of the first psychologists to assign developmental stages to adolescence and young adulthood. He defined development by stages of psychosocial crisis, which also could be defined as stages of transition. Of the eight stages the two critical ones for our college age students are identity versus identity confusion and intimacy versus isolation. Identity is the individual's self-examination and answer to the question "Who am I?' Successful resolution of this stage is acquiring a self-awareness that includes an understanding and commitment to one's values. Your student may explore and finalize these values during his college years. One young woman became very interested in the Jewish faith and during her quest found a Jewish boyfriend. She began to attend the Hillel activities on campus and celebrated the Jewish holidays with her boyfriend's family. Whether or not she will convert and/or marry this young man is yet to be determined, but she is in a heady time of exploration and learning, which is important to her development. This exploration is frequently very difficult for parents to understand and especially accept because the results may contradict the family's values. A student looks at his choice of major/occupation, religion, politics and sexual behavior. Lack of resolution results in a state of confusion about who he is or for what he stands. These confused individuals are easily swayed and frequently adopt the values of others, changing values with any change of acquaintances.

The second stage of Erikson's hierarchy of development affecting college age students is the psychosocial stage of intimacy versus isolation. The challenge of this transition is learning how to relate to others. Although this stage addresses emotional and sexual intimacy, it also applies to the tolerance of others who may be different from self. What better laboratory for exploring relationships than a college campus and particularly first year residence halls where students are randomly assigned to both living quarters and roommates? Unsuccessful resolution of this stage, not learning how to relate to others, would result in the isolation of the student from others. Erikson's theory states that attaining independence and autonomy is a critical aspect of achieving identity. The overall goal of any well-trained college administrator is the emergence of an independent and educated adult.

Arthur Chickering, in his famous work *Education and Identity* (1969), expanded the theory of the psychosocial development of college students by dividing the stage of identity development into seven vectors that he arranged in a chronological hierarchy. The first three occur simultaneously in the early college years. They include developing competence, managing emotions, and developing autonomy leading to the fourth vector - establishing identity. Following the establishment of identity, the student proceeds through the final three vectors of freeing interpersonal relationships, developing purpose and developing integrity. Thus in the first years, students are working on developing competence which includes everything from academic achievement to washing one's clothes without turning all the whites to pink from a stray red sock. Students also set out to learn to control their emotions. He may learn not to put his fist through the door when he is angry or she may learn to staunch the endless flow of tears when a friendship ends. According to this theory, a student must also achieve autonomy primarily from parents in order to proceed to establish his identity. Both Erickson and Chickering define identity as a state of independence.

Later theorists including Carol Gilligan (1982) approached psychological development from a feminist viewpoint. In a woman's development of identity, she would strive to maintain relationships with others not to separate. As we look at the movement of developmental psychology to a model of emerging adulthood, the role of relationships takes precedence over the earlier ideals of independence and autonomy. Josselson (1987) suggested that achieving identity might best be served by a continued connection between parent and child in conjunction with separation. Our college age student's goals are to stay connected to family and friends and to rely on others while allowing others to rely on the student at the same time.

Consulting

The current trend toward a continuing relationship between parents and their young adults is best understood and best served by a model of transition from a parent-child to an adult-adult relationship. Parents consulting and guiding their students through emerging adulthood can accomplish this new relationship. The goal is a combination of an independent and related identity for the young adult. For the parent, the goal is an adult-to-adult relationship that reflects both the autonomous independence of Erickson and Chickering and the connectedness of Gilligan and Josselson. Students who continue under their parents' tight tutelage do not grow into independent adults. I believe it is essential for your student to use the college years to develop not only intellectually but also emotionally and socially.

In your role as a consultant to your son you want to provide him with good advice based on your life experiences and education and your knowledge and understanding of the resources that are available to him on campus (see Appendix A for a list of usual services on a college campus). Students who use college services are more successful, healthier and happier. Students won't always say, "Thank you. I will make an appointment tomorrow." Nor do your consultees always take your advice. Plant the seed with information, water and warm with encouragement and sometimes your student will take advantage of the available assistance.

I recommend gates in your fences so your daughter can wander into adjoining pastures and back home again. Leave the gate open by asking questions and being interested but continue to profess your own values. It is important to tolerate her mistakes and still lend support rather than communicate an "I told you so." If it is right for your daughter, she will return to your pasture. If you slam the gate by being extremely critical, condemning or even disowning her, you will make it much more difficult for her to return to your values or to continue a relationship with you.

As a high school guidance counselor, I often discuss with parents the importance of acknowledging the transition from high school to college, and the need to prepare their children for this event well before the end of their high school days. I will often use the term "collective bargaining" when discussing with parents the form this process will resemble. The student wants more independence, freedom or responsibility, and the parents desire proof that their child is ready for these additional liberties-often through a greater contribution to the household. I believe it is critical that parents encourage this give-and-take, but warn that the process is seldom seamless. High school adolescents experimenting with adult roles fluctuate frequently between childlike and adult behavior; it is simply the way of young people in the maturation process. Success in this "bargaining" should bring rewards, and shortcomings accountability. However, each time the child makes an attempt at more adult behaviors, regardless of outcome, it should be viewed as an opportunity for reflection, self-assessment, and parent-child communication.

Andy Scappattici, M.Ed.
High School Counselor
Quakertown Pennsylvania

As a college student, I often remember calling home to receive advice about which classes to take, whether to rush a sorority, which extracurricular activities to choose and daily decisions in my college life. I appreciated advice but never controlling opinions. I appreciated when my mom after listening to all aspects would help me to decide for myself. She never told me what to do nor did she try to control my decisions. She listened to my thoughts and helped me to make my own decisions. My mom also supported me in the decisions I made. She was neither critical nor judgmental. There were times I didn't ask for advice. When advice was given in this manner, I valued it, rather than resenting it. Jessica

When I went to college, everything was changing: my home, my friends, myself. Parents usually seem to understand this. However, they don't always understand the impact this change has on their relationship with their child. The child is now becoming an adult and the transition is gradual, exciting, and at times very painful. It took a very long time to figure out where my parents fit in my newly forming life. It is wonderful to realize that you can begin to see your parents as real people and communicate with them on more intellectual levels.

However, it gets confusing to a young adult what role they want their parents to play. College students begin to assume the role of power that their parents have always had. They begin to put up their own fences to help maintain their developing independence. Parents must respect these boundaries and not take them personally. Believe me, there were plenty of times I pushed my parents away when I really wanted to run into the comfort of the old days, when they were in charge.

I could tell sometimes my distance hurt them and I wanted to tell them that it was hurting me as well. But I usually didn't give them any explanations and I really needed my parents not to ask them of me. Sometimes things became too overwhelming and I would concede to ask for help. If you know your children well, trust them to come for you when the time is right. Kristina

Chapter 2   The Cornerstone - Communications

1. **Listen to the content**

2. **Listen to the emotion/affect**

3. **Reflect back to your student**

4. **Now offer advice, maybe**

5. **Clearly communicate your needs**

6. **Reinforce desired behavior**

7. **Offer physical and verbal affection**

8. **Make sure the time and place are right**

9. **Say it only once**

10. **Send packages, snail mail and email**

11. **Make your mail supportive and positive**

12. **Let your student determine the frequency of phone contact**

Realistically this whole book is about communication, as are all human relationships, but I think it is important that the how, what, when, where and why of communication deserve a chapter. Communication is the cornerstone for your relationship with your college bound student.

You have been communicating with your student for approximately eighteen years. You know your daughter's willingness to share information and emotions with you and her ability to listen to you. Make sure that you listen to the content and the affect/emotion and reflect back to your daughter what you hear before you offer advice. For example if your daughter calls to tell you what an idiot her roommate, teacher, coach, or you fill in the blank is, it is important to make sure that you understand what happened and let your daughter know that you understand what she is feeling – embarrassment, anger, disappointment? Only after your daughter has clarified the incident and expressed her feelings can she move on to solving the problem and, maybe, listening to your input.

How to communicate

Believe it or not the first rule about communication is not about what you say but how you listen. What can you do if your son won't talk? Often we need to prime the pump with open-ended questions that require more than a yes or no answer. Instead of "Did you have a good time at the party?" or "Is your homework done?" we might want to ask, "What did you like about the party?" or "Tell me about the homework assignment that you were working on."

Once you or your son have started the conversation, it is important to listen actively. Active listening as described by Gordon (1975) means hearing what your son says by concentrating first on the content and secondly on the affect, or emotion, of your son's statements. Also your verbal and physical behavior should encourage the continuation of the dialogue/monologue. Head nodding, uh huh's, and repeating a word or phrase or occasionally summarizing what you are hearing should keep your son talking for a while. What you don't want to do is listen with one ear tuned to your son and the other tuned to your reactions and responses in your own head. Many of us ostensibly listen while we are really rehearsing what we are going to say when the other person stops speaking. We miss much of the content and usually all of the affect when we do this. You have listened effectively if you can repeat back to your son the essence of his words to his satisfaction. Check yourself by saying, "John, I heard you say that the calculus exam was on material that wasn't covered in class and you are feeling misled. Am I correct?" John may correct you because you got it wrong but he also may correct you as he continues to revise his thinking. If you are a consultant at a company the first thing you want to do is actively, there's that word again, seek the opinions of the workers before proposing plans and solutions. Finding out what your son thinks will guide your response.

Your son may get mail from his newly selected college that fateful pre-college summer. You are anxious for him to open the letter and share with you the news of his dorm assignment, roommate's name or class registration. He comes home from his summer job at the pool and when you hand him his letter he says, "Later," leaving the letter on the foyer table. What is going on here? Your son may feel anxious about the change coming in his life and wants to avoid even thinking about it. You might respond to his behavior by reflecting his feelings. "John you seem uninterested in your college plans. Perhaps you are feeling anxious?" This is an example of reading the affect behind the words.

Another example might be when your daughter, who does open that housing letter, starts to cry. She has been assigned a triple in the oldest and only single sex residence hall on campus with a girl from New York City and a foreign student. She wanted a double in a coed dorm with a girl she knows from summer camp. She is upset and dissatisfied because her expectations weren't met. You want to allow her to vent and explain further. In this case the real cause of her upset may possibly be the apprehension of sharing a room after 18 years as an only child who didn't have to share anything. Again you hear the content and the affect. "You seem upset by your rooming assignment."

A rising sophomore recently told me about her first semester on campus. She was placed in a quad, in the damp basement of an all-female dorm. She has allergies and immediately put in a request for a room change to a dryer double. So I asked her if she eventually changed her living environment that first semester. She responded no that she quickly became friends with the other women, and, in spite of her allergies, she didn't want to move when the opportunity was offered. Her allergies were a real problem but her real motivation to move was the anxiety of the new and unknown. Active listening includes the art of hearing both the content and the affect that your daughter is communicating. Active listening should always be the preferred mode of communication when your daughter has a problem.

Another skill of communication is saying what you want to say or clearly communicating your needs. We are all very capable of having conversations with people for whom we care when there are no problems. We call these interchanges conversations because they are an exchange of information and this is the mode you want to use most of the time when you are consulting on emerging adulthood with your son. During these times neither you nor your son have a problem and communication can be relatively carefree, informative, comfortable and open.

When your son's behavior is unacceptable and you want to tell him so is often the time when communication becomes difficult. This is the time when we need to let our son know how we feel. It often takes us a minute or two or more to recognize our true feelings. Most of us are quick to identify what our son is doing that upsets us, but to understand and identify our own emotional response takes thoughtful inquiry. Whenever I ask others to identify what they are feeling, they initially respond with what they think.

For example, if you feel angry that your son didn't return your phone calls for three weeks, you might say, "I feel that you should return my phone calls." The problem with this statement is that beginning with the word "you" immediately puts your son on the defensive because you are making an accusation and telling him what to do. Instead you want to identify your feeling at the time, which actually may not be the quickly identified anger but a feeling of disappointment. Thus when we communicate with our son we want to model the importance of conveying emotion by saying, "I feel disappointed that you have not returned my calls for the last three weeks." Gordon (1975) calls this form of communication an "I message." After expressing your feelings and your son's specific behavior, you can let him know what you would like him to do instead. "I would like you to return a phone call from me within twenty-four hours." This is the same message but offered by a different approach that your son is more likely to hear. This communication is more likely to evoke a response rather than a retort.

When we wish to communicate negative messages it is very important to think about our goal or purpose in communicating these negative feelings to our daughter. Is our goal to get her to change her behavior? This is a very difficult goal to accomplish. She is an adult and she is in charge of her behavior. She can do what she pleases, particularly since you aren't around to check up on her. Is our goal to make her feel guilty about not doing what we want her to do? Guilt has been a mother's tool for centuries. "I am not telling you what to do but I won't rest if I know you are no longer attending church." But what are the consequences of guilt? One of the initial consequences of guilt is shame. One feels shame when doing something that people who love us don't want us to do. Shame is not a useful emotion. Notice we are feeling shame while we are doing the disapproved behavior. So guilt doesn't change the behavior, it just adds a new feeling to your daughter's emotional repertoire. Think about what happens when you feel guilty. Maybe you have changed your behavior but typically the next emotion is resentment. "All right I did what you wanted me to do but I am really unhappy about it and I am really angry at you." Yes, we may have attained our goal of a behavior change, but at what price?

The most useful way to set the stage for behavior change is to consult. Being a consultant means giving her information that may be helpful to her in choosing to behave in a way that we think would be more advantageous. If you were asked to consult at a company, you would not try to change behaviors by applying guilt or punishment. You would offer information to be used in the company's decision-making process that might persuade them to try things your way. Persuasion is the important modality. You want to offer her information that she may use to change her behavior and you want to persuade her to change.

B. F. Skinner (1953) himself said punishment doesn't change behavior as effectively as reinforcement does. Using the benefits of positive and negative reinforcement of desired behavior can influence your daughter. Positive reinforcement includes praise, approval, recognition, and reward. Praising your daughter's continued attendance at Sunday services is more effective than condemning her interest in a Zen meditation group. Negative reinforcement includes the removal of adverse stimuli. If your daughter finds dorm living to be distracting and repressive, the permission to live at home or the money for an off campus living environment can be negative reinforcement for better studying by removing the negative stimulus of dorm living. Reinforcement needs to directly follow the performance of the desired behavior, whether improved grades or completing her application for a summer internship.

What to communicate

Person-to-person communication is the best way to convey your love and respect for your student. When my daughters were young, we often included one or more of their friends on family vacations or at special events. I often found that my children really enjoyed sharing our family life with their friends and changing the sibling dynamics by adding others. Darlene, one of Jess's friends, often came with us and was surprised by the frequent verbal and physical affection between my daughters and I. I don't think a day has gone by when I haven't told my daughters I loved them nor a night gone by without a goodnight hug and kiss. Darlene went home to her mother and said, "Why don't you ever tell me that you love me?" Her mother responded, "What do you mean?" Darlene responded, "Mrs. W. tells Jess she loves her all the time?" "You know I do." "But I want to hear you say it."

It is very important for your daughter to hear you say it, especially during this most vulnerable time when she is struggling with her self-worth and lovability. Although you at times may not approve of her behavior, she needs to know that you will never stop loving and believing in her. If not you than who will offer her such love? One important, if not the most important factor in healthy ego development is your student's knowing that there is at least one person in this world who loves her unconditionally so that she too can unconditionally love herself.

So any time you are communicating with your daughter it is important, in your own style, and you may not be the huggy, feeling type like me, to offer physical and verbal affection to your daughter. Don't confuse my encouragement of expressing positives to your daughter with the management/supervision training style of offering a compliment before you confront someone with the true purpose of your communication – negative feedback. The positive is not the introduction to the negative. Positives should stand-alone and underlie any communication with your daughter.

When to communicate

Another aspect of communication is timing. When your daughter will be able to hear you and when she will not hear you is based on timing. Her mood or alertness at the time may determine her openness to your communication. I describe the times when my younger daughter allows me to tell her things as "open door moments." At those times I can walk into her mind and say most anything and get a thoughtful response. Other times I would approach the door only to find it locked or even slammed in my face. At these times all my exhortations are in vain. It is much better to have conversations when the door is open and the welcome mat is out. In business we wouldn't think of delivering our consultation report when there is a crises at the company or it is a holiday. When the consultee is ready to listen is the time to present the report and often this means an appointment. You can make a time and place to discuss issues with your daughter or be more spontaneous if your approach is met in a welcoming manner.

Another warning for parents is to say it only once. In a recent conversation with other parents of "twenty somethings," we admitted to the tendency to make our point repeatedly thinking maybe we weren't really heard or feeling impressed with our skill at making our point and wanting to repeat it. If you have this urge, resist it. Don't wait for the signal of your son's drawing his finger across his throat suggesting that you cut the lecture. Be glad you were able to make your point and move on. This is not a good time for repetition. If your son's behavior reflects a lack of understanding your point, you can introduce the concept again at another time.

Where to communicate

Communication in person includes more information than all other modes. When we are with each other, we have all the body cues of emotional reactions to our words – facial expressions, nearness to each other, voice tone, position of arms, etc. Research shows that our reliance on the Internet is interfering with the development of the skills that allow us to read the physical responses and body language of others. The advantage of our parent-student relationship is that we have done the majority of our communication with each other in person over the years. Communicating with our now independent student now includes different types of interactions. When problems are serious or feelings are intense, a face-to-face conversation will provide the best information and interaction.

Also we need the right time and space to have a conversation that won't be interrupted by the usual daily activities. I have found over the years that car talk is a most effective form of communication. Both individuals look straight ahead, which provides some physical restriction to the intimacy. Neither party can get out of the moving car to avoid the conversation. In addition to car talk these conversations can take place over the dinner table or before bedtime, whenever natural conversation happens in your family.

Modes of communication

Mail

Communication as a skill is an important topic but the actual means of communication is also important in advising your son. In today's world there are many modes of communication. How does one stay in touch? This is a tricky topic. It is difficult to maneuver between finding out what is happening in your daughter's life and your daughter's need for independence and privacy. A great way to stay in touch with your child is to send lots of cards and letters stuffed with relevant clippings. I remember being at camp with a classmate in our junior high years. Her mother sent us daily notes and clippings from the weekly hometown paper. We looked forward to these daily news briefs and appreciated the touch of home when we were away. It is hard to imagine in this day of instant messaging (IM'ing) and email that "snail mail" would matter. I still have a never ending, repetitive dream about walking down the circular stairway in my college union, anticipating my pre-lunch mail call. In the dream, I approach the traditional mailboxes at the bottom of the stairs only to find that I can't remember my mailbox combination. There is mail in the box and the mailroom clerks behind the wall of small glass doors ignore my pleas for them to hand me the mail in my box. The repetition of this dream into middle age demonstrates the importance of mail in the life of the college student. Mail is so highly prized that not being able to get to it is like being separated from one's family and friends. The mailboxes at my alma mater haven't changed and it is still a matter of pride for an alum to saunter up to his old box and, remembering the combination, unlock the box to his college communications. Students still swarm around the campus mailboxes around the lunch hour. Just the other day I saw a student taking a photograph of his college mailbox, maybe for a class assignment or a college senior's scrapbook. Today there are recycle bins that collect the junk mail, usually mail sent by the administration or faculty. Real mail is cards and letters with stamps from you and other loved ones.

Another recommendation – make your mail supportive and not negative. Mail is now and always was a major communication tool for parents. In college we would gather around the lunch table to chuckle over the ranting of one friend's mother. Letters from naïve mother Claire amused and entertained us with her tirades about all the ills of current college students. However, there was no humor when years later at a mini college reunion, one of my other college friends came across a very critical letter from her mother. The five of us gathered at a friend's home had all brought our box of college mementos. It is amazing how the multiple boxes of the contents of your senior college dorm room shrink to one box over the years. Nancy pulled a letter from her mother out of her box of a freshman beanie, a florist card that had accompanied valentine flowers and sorority formal photos, and she read the letter aloud:

"Dear Nancy, I just wanted to let you know how very disappointed I am in you. I am very upset at your choice of a boyfriend from outside our religious beliefs. You are throwing your father and my values in our face. To think that you are having sex with this boy is outside the standards of common human decency and of your good upbringing. I am ashamed to call you my daughter and don't know if I can ever forgive you."

We greeted the reading of this 20-year-old letter with silence, unable to say the right thing. At this time Nancy's mother had been dead for over 10 years. There is no opportunity to undo these hurtful words or resolve the bad feelings between mother and daughter. At this same reunion there was a letter from my mother in my box. It was brief and included words of love and support although it followed a period when I had been subjected to disciplinary action for being in a male dorm after hours.

I am not saying don't give negative feedback to your child. What I am saying is don't put it in writing for her to pull out of a box 20 years from now. Dramatic? Yes, but also true.

Perhaps a more common scenario is your son's F on the midterm report makes you angry and you immediately think that he is wasting your money. It seems like a good idea at the time to put your pen to paper or fingers to the keyboard to let him know what you are feeling. DON'T DO IT!! Although it may make you feel better at the moment, there is a time delay between the time that you reach catharsis by writing, stamping, and sending the letter or clicking the send button and the moment when he opens his combination mail box or email. He receives your message with your return address after he has just failed the Calc I test and his girlfriend just went out with his roommate. "Yea! A letter from home to cheer me up and make me feel better about life." Surprise!!!

Negative feedback is best done in person when both parties are calm. Make the negative feedback part of a conversation where you can share your concerns and negative feelings and hear their thoughts about their behavior and your reaction.

Care packages are always welcome. Particularly food. Are you sending your homemade chocolate chip cookies? I often wonder about the thrift of spending $3.98 on mailing a package of jellybeans that cost me 99 cents but the pleasure of my daughter immediately erases the budgetary concerns.

Email

That wonderful (?) invention. I think email was specifically created for parents; one-way communication with your college student who never seems to be in his room and never returns your voice mail messages. Email is an opportunity to communicate with your son about everything from daily events to good advice about his sore throat. Just don't expect a reply. The biggest use of computer time on college campuses is email. Just like the messages that you left on his answering machine, he doesn't have to respond or even acknowledge receiving your message. Try the automatic receipt option so you can know if he even opened it. Email is like adding a drop of water into the ocean. You may not know the effect of that single drop of water but in the end it is part of that ocean of parental advice that flows in waves over your student for use at some future moment. She is also likely to open it when she is most receptive to reading what you have written unlike the ill timed phone call with information that falls on deaf ears. Have you ever gotten a letter in the mail that may be bearing negative news and let it lay on the foyer table until you are emotionally and mentally prepared to open it and read it? Email is also a good way of forwarding articles and opportunities from the World Wide Web or others. Those greeting cards are rarely opened and remember you are competing with all her friends for her on-line attention. I guarantee that from time to time you will receive from your daughter assorted chain letters promising gift certificates at teen adored stores. After all you are part of her address book.

Do's and Do Not's of Email

Do send email
Do provide an interesting subject line
Don't expect a response
Don't send electronic greeting cards

Telephone

So far, the record cost for a telephone bill for the first month of school is $300. I am sure there are those of you reading this book that can top this record. By the way, this student was not calling mom and dad but her friends who had gone to college all over the United States. Even though there are 5 cents a minute Sundays, students call when they want or need to talk to their friends or you. Many of them have spent their high school years communicating on the telephone but then it was all included in that unlimited local fee. So what does this mean for parent-student communication? Most students would prefer that you call them because then you pay for it and they never see the bill. Most upper class students settle into a routine whether it is every Sunday or every day at a prearranged time when you call them and they will be in their room to receive your call.

Telephone communication is important to both you and your student.

The best thing my parents did for me was to be available and unoffended when I was unavailable. I know I can call my parents whenever and talk to them about school, jobs, friends, money and they will be there but they are never offended when I say I can't talk or I don't want to talk about whatever. They understand that college is when kids don't want their parents interfering and that we want to figure out what to do on our own. To do the switch from parenting to advising without being authoritative is imperative to the relationship. It all hinges on communication.

Morgan senior

Whether your son calls multiple times in the first few days or not at all for the first few weeks, you should know that there are all kinds of phone arrangements between student and parent. A wise parent communicates about communication. "Do you want me to call?" "When do you want me to call?" "How often do you want me to call?"

Cell phones have changed all the rules. Students are attached to cell phones everywhere and anytime. It is still important to examine your own rules of cell phone use and pass them on to your student. Cell phones do not belong in the classroom setting. Anything can wait for the 50 - 75 minutes class and if not the student should consider missing class altogether. Do you talk on your phone in your car, at the dinner table, walking down the street, at a party, etc? I am sure for some of you the answer is yes. I encourage your student to limit his cell phone use. Remember what it was like to experience life in the moment without the annoying interruption of someone else. Use the general guidelines for phone use in this chapter and if you want to call or are receiving numerous cell phone calls to or from your student, ask yourself why?

Sometimes your student saves all the angst for you. If you were a fly on the wall you may see him eating pizza and watching football on television with his hallmates right after he called you to tell you how much he hates this college. Part of the reality is that your listening serves as a release valve for his anxiety and negative feelings. It is unnecessary for you to get involved in resolving the distress; merely listen to him vent. When my daughter was little she would follow every piano lesson with an "I hate piano and I am never going back." My initial reaction was the desire to deny her response and say, "No you don't really hate playing piano. Maybe it was just a hard lesson today, or maybe if you practiced more you would play better and enjoy your lesson more." I soon learned that it was unnecessary for me to get involved in resolving her distress. The more effective strategy was to merely listen to her vent. An active listening response would be, "It sounds like you are frustrated with your piano lesson today." Of course she would go back the next week and to this day appreciates her piano playing skill. Remember to reflect content and affect. So you might say, "It sounds like you are upset that you feel like you haven't made any real friends at your college." Content – lack of friends and affect – upset are part of good communication.

What if your daughter is calling several times per day? Most importantly you want to stay positive when your daughter calls. Listen to her concerns and reflect back her upsetting emotions. But don't contribute to her emotions with your own anxiety. Encourage her to get involved in an activity. In those early weeks, clubs are just getting organized and are actively pursuing new members. Your daughter should be able to find something she likes to do which will mean being with others who also like to do what she finds interesting. Encourage her to attend meals. If she cannot find someone to accompany her, she should ask her resident advisor or student advisor to attend a meal with her. Also encourage her to get some physical activity perhaps at the life sports center by walking, swimming, lifting weights etc. This will also get her out of the residence hall and into a place where there are other students. Finally you should plan with her to modify her behavior by reducing the number of phone calls home per day by a steadily decreasing amount. If your daughter is calling you 6 times a day, at the end of the day say, "You know we have spoken 6 times today and I think it would be a good idea if we spoke only 5 times tomorrow." If you do that for 5 days, the phone calls will be down to a more acceptable number. If your daughter is homesick and that is why she is calling you several times a day, this is interfering with her spending time at activities getting to know other students. Also moving calls to mid day or late afternoon will help diminish homesickness. It is important for the student to engage in her day at the college in the morning without emotionally connecting to home and the resulting sadness.

Many female students do communicate with their mother on a daily basis. This depends on your relationship and your daughter's needs. Please note I said your daughter's needs, not yours. This is one of the most important paradoxes of the college years. It is important for your daughter to stay attached to you and separate from you. Frequently when our daughter is experiencing this transition, we too are experiencing transitions in our life. It might be a particular difficult time in our career, a newly empty nest, a divorce, the care/death of our aging parents or a change in our own health. As a single mother I experienced more loneliness and empty space in my life after my younger daughter left for school. But it is important to find other support systems to deal with our emotional angst. Your daughter is dealing with a particularly stressful time of growth in her life and taking care of Mom or Dad should not be on her list. It is, therefore, important to let your daughter determine the frequency of contact by phone during those early months. Sometimes it's not only moms who get impatient with the lack of calls from their college student.

yes, dad, of course I miss you! but not when you leave messages on my voice mail after I haven't talked to you for 3 days, that say "Hello dear, this is your father, remember me? I wanted to say hi, please call home if you have time, the number is." and you leave our home phone number. The number I memorized 15 year ago when me moved in.daaaaaaaaaaad uuuuuuuuuuuugggh.

> (or) mom, chill, i miss you too.
> Kerin junior

Interestingly, I have met several young women in counseling whose mothers decided to pursue romantic relationships now that the children were out of the nest. Several of these young women were feeling jealousy and rejection now that they weren't the center of their mothers' worlds. Transitions can be difficult and must be undertaken with care for everyone's feelings.

Telephone communication may go to the other extreme – no phone calls at all. On the opening day of college orientation, one young woman with her parents in tow found her way to my counseling office. Home was a 10-hour drive away. Dad was ready to hit the road but neither Mom nor daughter could separate. Both were crying. Mom finally tore herself away and Mandy with tear stained face waved good-bye as Dad pulled the car from the curb. One of the things I have learned as a counselor is that I can't predict human behavior. Mandy didn't call her parents nor answer their calls for three weeks. Of course the parents were beside themselves with worry. When asked to explain her behavior, Mandy said, "I knew if I had any contact with them, I would experience the same upset I felt on that first day so I decided to go cold turkey. It was the only way I could adjust to my new surroundings without succumbing to homesickness."

Mandy's solution is unusual but the reality is that there are all kinds of phone arrangements between student and parent. A wise parent communicates about communication. That doesn't mean that you won't still get that phone call at the wrong time - in the middle of the night when you are sound asleep, in the morning right before you leave for a stressful day at the office or at the end of the day. There is your daughter on the other end of the line needing your listening ear about her moody roommate, unfaithful boyfriend or unreasonable faculty member.

Why communicate

There are several purposes of communication that we may not have clarified. Communication is the way we maintain our old relationship with the child we sent to college. It is also the way we establish a new relationship with the adult our student is becoming. We show our mutual respect for each other. And finally communication just may ease our worry as we allow our student to move into the new fields of emerging adulthood.

It is important for parents to listen to their child instead of trying to fix the problem. Realistically, a parent cannot fix their child's problems nor should they. The student needs to figure out how to help solve the problem and at times will need a parent to listen. Jessica

Letters, emails, phone calls, smoke signals...do what works best between you and your daughter. During my years at college, it varied widely. When I was in prep school, I used email all the time and that was how I communicated with my parents. But I found quickly that what you write on your end isn't always read the same on the other end. I had been writing my parents to ask about going on a road trip with friends to see a concert. They had written back that they were not wild about the idea but they were willing to discuss it. I was discouraged and decided to write a joking email to lighten up the serious tone they had taken. I remember writing something like, "I object. I am beyond your jurisdiction; I am in New Jersey now and yours ends at the state border of Pennsylvania." I was just joking around, but it turns out my dad had taken me literally. Luckily my mom called me and told me how my email had come across, and she gave me a chance to explain myself.

Emails are usually a good way to communicate but they are no place for serious issues. I've never been a fan of phone calls. I've had many conversations with my parents about not calling as much as they do. The worst thing for me is the answering machine. My mom and dad used to deal with the machine very differently. My mom would leave messages telling me she was thinking of me and loved me and that I didn't have to call her back. But my dad tended to leave more than one message, each one getting progressively more disappointed or upset. This made me feel very guilty but it does not make me call him back. In fact I would often be annoyed and avoid future phone calls from him. It took a while to figure out the phone situation. It took a few years of mishaps until junior year when I finally explained exactly how I felt about his calls. We decided he should only call once a week. I was free to call whenever I wanted and from time to time I did, and those conversations were much more animated and enjoyable because they were on my terms. Kristina

Chapter 3   The Student Challenge - Managing Time

1. **Buy your student a planner**
2. **Talk about the way you organize your time**
3. **Request a time audit**
4. **Model a healthy life schedule**

Every year I hear the same thing from seasoned college students. The major hurdle to college adjustment in the first year is an inability to manage time. The new college student is bewildered by the lack of externally imposed structure.

A typical high school day

In high school, our children get up at a specific time. To take care of her daily toiletry needs, my daughter got up hours before the school bus arrived. They get on the bus or they drive off to school. The school day is organized by a class schedule. Free periods are often supervised - a study hall or an assigned activity. The school bell rings at the end of the day and the high school student moves on to an after school sport, job, or activity. There may be a family dinner hour determined by when mom or dad or someone is able to make dinner. After dinner there are more activities, homework, phone time and a little television. The family probably goes to bed at a fairly reasonable hour depending on your morning schedule for the following day and your son's need to get up and be at high school probably between 7 and 8 a.m. The week probably also includes the structure of family chores and weekends include more of the same activities - jobs, friends, sports and religious services.

As my younger daughter learned, boarding school is even more restrictive with prescribed evening study halls, lights out at bedtime, restricted hours for the wall phone or lobby television and even Saturday classes. I thought her college adjustment would be very easy after living away from home for two years, but as she pointed out to me, college life was the opposite end from boarding school on the restriction continuum with home rules falling somewhere in the middle.

The college wake-up call

So what happens when this normal high school student arrives at college? The first thing he notices is that he is probably only taking four or five courses and he only goes to class two or three times a week per course. This means that he has a total class time of 10 to 15 hours compared to the normal high school week of 37 hours. The summer before they enter college, many students and their parents think they should take more courses because this certainly is less than their high school demands. First year students are frequently stunned by the expectation that they should spend two to three hours out of class for every hour in class. This would be a minimum 45-hour academic workweek and if your son followed this schedule he would probably make dean's list (usually an A-/A average). So for his first, second and even third week of college, he goes to his minimal 10 to 15 hours of classes. He stays up very late at night and complains about how difficult it is to get up for an 8 or 9 a.m. class. Remember only a few short months ago he arose at 6 a.m. to make sure he was showered before the bus came at 7:00. Now he attends that first class

50

unshowered and unfed wearing his pajama bottoms, sweatshirt and backward baseball cap. He immediately returns to bed after that first class and gets up in time for lunch that lasts for 90 minutes in the snack bar. He may be showered for that 1:30 class but returns to the dorm to change before leaving for his basketball preseason weightlifting session in the gym. He showers again and goes back to the dining hall for dinner. Maybe, he will spend a little time reading before sitting down to watch the Monday night football game with his buddies followed by pizza and beer and hanging out. Managing one's time is absolutely one of the major challenges facing first year students.

The most important thing a new student should do is get into a routine so he/she will get all the work and classes done every day. I found that this works best for me. After classes I will lift weights to get exercise and unwind a little, then either go to the library or my room to start doing work. Once I am finished with work, I will then relax. I find if I take a nap after classes that I will become tired and hold off my work till late in the night.

Leigh junior

How to help – buy a planner

How can you help? First and foremost all college students should have a planner. Buy one today. This planner can be any form they like. A bound paper product or a small handheld computer product that they know how to use is the best for writing down classes, assignments, appointments and social obligations. Students who start the first day with this planner and use it will be more successful at managing their time and accomplishing the tasks at hand. It is important when your children are in high school to also encourage them to use planners and assignment books and talk to them about the way you organize your time. Share with them the kind of planning calendar that you use and the kinds of things that you document on that calendar, whether it is the way you run your home, your office or both.

Create a schedule

Let's look at your planner. What do you include in your daily, weekly or monthly schedule? First of all we put down our work schedule. When are you working in and out of the workplace? Your daughter's schedule building will also start with her work – in class and out of class time (studying). Projects we are working on and their deadlines for completion are inherent to formulating our work schedule. The student should take her syllabus and mark all test dates and due dates for papers and projects. The goal is to be able to quickly see at a glance what is coming the next day, week or month.

Another excellent aspect of planners is the space for lists. Anyone who has taken time management training knows the value of lists – goals and objectives. Also the "to do's" should be prioritized. This is particularly advantageous to students who have many long-term assignments. If they accomplish the items on their "to do list" on a daily basis, the 20 page end-of-term paper will get done in phases rather than in a rush at the last minute. I frequently take a large pad of paper and list all my tasks. I even include the ones I have just finished to immediately experience a sense of completion and accomplishment as I cross off these tasks. Your daughter should break that semester-long term paper into chunks - checking the library for primary source books, ordering articles from interlibrary loan, making note cards of bibliographical references, etc. Such a road map of small tasks for the student to do every day keeps her motivated by her sense of accomplishment and allows her to get the large task done.

Do a time audit

Your son earns less than a 2.0 cumulative average at mid term reports. His excuse is that he has no time to study. What to do? Have him do a time audit. What have we learned from those efficiency experts? Most of us waste time. How do we learn about how we spend our time? How do we keep track of our activities? Ask your son to write down what he is doing every 15 minutes for 24-48 hours to establish a baseline of how he spends his time. I can guarantee that if he is honest, he will find that he is losing time with meaningless tasks. When he thinks he is studying for two hours, he will be surprised to find all the extraneous things that interrupt that time - the friend who stops in for a chat, the phone call from home, the trips to change the laundry from the washer to the dryer. After he does this audit, you will need to say very little because the truth will be self-evident. After doing his time audit, he can return to his schedule with a new awareness of the difference between what we plan to do and what we really do with our time.

Prioritize activities

The next category on our schedule might be the time we spend with family, loved ones and friends. This is social time and is also necessary for college students. Whether it is hanging out in the dorm or spending time with her boyfriend, your daughter needs social time built into her schedule. Sometimes this social time is unscheduled and overruns all her free time. I well remember my first semester at college when I loved the idea of living in a dorm with so many potential friends. I would enter a room and hang out. When the room occupants decided it was time to get back to their books, I would wander to the next room and interrupt their studying for some social time. I dubbed myself the walking study break. It really was no surprise when I earned a 1.8 (out of 4.0) for my first semester grade point average. If I wasn't socializing in the dorms, I was sitting at lunch playing bridge for 2 hours or chatting in the library looking for party leads. So allowing some social time that is limited will avoid a fulltime social schedule with other more important activities squeezed in between.

A good time for socializing is mealtime. Most first year students are on a meal plan and therefore don't have to allow time for meal preparation, food shopping etc that occupy our daily routine. She does still need time to wash her clothes, clean her room, and attend to her toiletries. This is one area many students let slide without you around to urge (nag) them.

A word about extracurricular activities

We might also find time on our schedule for a variety of activities including recreational, religious and volunteer opportunities. And the extracurricular activities at college are also important. These activities are the source of some of the most valuable learning experiences by enhancing the classroom learning or providing opportunities for physical or emotional development. Running an organization, serving at a Shabbat dinner, being captain of her intramural soccer team, writing for the newspaper, serving on a women's crises hotline are all activities that warrant time on your daughter's schedule. Also, involved students are the happiest students. When do you feel that your life is most fulfilled? For many of us, life satisfaction comes from the activities that we engage in outside of our workday world. The greatest concern for first year students is under or over involvement. The student who doesn't engage in her favorite activities on campus may feel left out and bored. The student who takes on every activity that comes along may find it hard to accomplish her academic goals. Look at your own life. Do you follow a schedule that includes breathing, thinking or watching the flowers grow? You may very well have modeled a lifestyle that is difficult to live up to and dangerous to one's health. So as you advise your daughter, it might be time to reexamine your own priorities.

Free time

Free time for your student is an hour or two per day that remains available for any spontaneous needs. It might include extra study time for a test or a trip to the grocery store for snacks or an unexpected phone call from a friend. The idea is that there is some scheduled time that is unscheduled. Fun time is just what it sounds like. Whatever is fun for this particular student should be scheduled in to your son's schedule so he can maintain balance in his life. It is also very important for students to reward themselves for the accomplishment of small goals. When the goal for the day is reached, it is a great time to treat oneself with a favorite television program. We move forward in our life accomplishments by planning – setting and meeting goals and objectives Share how you accomplish everything from job assignments to redecorating your home by managing your time. Always remember to pay attention to your son's responses. There are times when he will welcome your advice and other times when he will not. Sometimes it is better to just stay silent.

Managing time was probably the most challenging concept to learn as a college freshman. There is so much free time that as a freshman it becomes easy to waste time. The transition from a rigorous high school schedule of 7-3 to a few hours per week of classes is difficult to adjust to at first. I soon learned that I needed to become more efficient in scheduling my day to make better use of my free time. I invested in a planner and tried to set a weekly schedule. I included time to relax, exercise and study. I found that by designating time slots for different activities, it helped me to make better use of my time. I soon leaned to adjust and enjoy my own schedule. Jessica

I was an atypical freshman. I was so nervous about doing well at an Ivy League School that I started my college career with a bang. I got a 3.7 my first semester. I don't know how I did it, except that I did not waste a minute of time. I was partying, sleeping, studying, or eating. It was a perfect balance that was bound to only last a semester or two. But it was a great way to start and I was able to maintain a more relaxed version of that lifestyle throughout the rest of college.

On the other hand, failing or withdrawing from a class or putting forth a minimal scholastic effort is very typical for a freshman. Most of the smartest and successful of my friends had a tough first semester and spent a good amount of their college career making up for it. As long as your daughter realizes that her education should be a top priority, then she will put the pressure on herself to raise her grades. My grades had ups and downs but pressure from my parents was nothing compared to the pressure I put on myself. If your daughter is responsible, your demands will be annoying rather than useful. But if you feel your daughter is falling way below her own expectations, it might be wise to broach the subject with her. Kristina

Chapter 4   It's Academic – A B G's

1. Advise your student to register for a reasonable number of classes
2. If your student wants to drop a course, listen to why
3. Don't write his papers
4. Encourage your student to go to class, talk to his professors and do his work
5. Remember the grades belong to your student, not you
6. Listen to the value of the grade according to your student
7. Speak to your student rather than call the faculty

After all, academics are what college is supposed to be all about, is it not?   We want our students to become educated. This chapter is about learning in the classroom, although I believe college is about intellectual growth in the classroom and through all other college experiences.

A semester of assignments

College academics pose a new challenge for your student. Some have experienced mediocre preparation in high school and find college to be difficult. Occasionally, a student enters a college where the course demands are less rigorous than in high school. She may actually reduce the time and energy she invests in her studies. Most of the time, a student finds college academics to be challenging.

First of all, students are expected to be more independent in managing their academic assignments. Typically a semester includes fifteen weeks of classes with in-class time averaging 2 1/2 to 4 hours per week plus lab time for the sciences. On the first day of class, a syllabus is distributed which outlines the dates for readings, tests, and papers plus the rules and regulations and contact information for that particular faculty member. The assignments are laid out for the entire semester and the syllabus may be the only communication from the professor regarding deadlines and dates. Students who are accustomed to high school teachers who give out such information in daily, weekly or unit doses can be overwhelmed by fifteen weeks of information provided all at one time. I have had students who have dropped my course the first day because the work presented all at one time outlined on the syllabus seemed too much to do in a semester. They forget that they can break it down into manageable units. Multiply four classes times 10 to 15 weeks of tests, papers and reading and the expected product would overwhelm any one of us.

How many courses?

The opposite phenomena is the student who is used to five or six major subjects in high school and wants to register for more courses than the number recommended by college policy. The summer before her entrance to college, Kristina wanted to sign up for more than four courses, the recommended first year load. As the semester progressed and the work demands seemed overwhelming, she was very glad to only have the original four courses. After a semester of adjustment, a heavier course load may be appropriate but not the first semester. It may also be advantageous for your student to register for classes with smaller enrollments. This will allow her to have more interaction with the professor and get more attention.

Dropping courses

Most colleges provide a brief time at the beginning of the semester for students to change their course registration. Students may be allowed to drop courses after a first look and add others in their place for the first seven to ten days of classes. After a longer period of time, students may still drop a course but are no longer able to add a course to replace it. After a few weeks there would just be too much work to catch up on. As the semester progresses a student may find that even the recommended number of courses are too much or one particular course is too difficult. Many a time, a student has met with me toward the 7th or 8th week of a semester to discuss dropping a course in which he is not doing well. Often we examine the pros and cons and reach a good educational decision. The next day the student returns and says his father says he can't drop the course because of money, time, or both. Although I appreciate the economic reality of receiving credit for only three courses instead of four and the possible need to attend summer school or even an additional semester, there is also the devastating effect on a grade point average (GPA) of that D or F in the first semester. I don't advocate dropping courses as a regular course of action to avoid low grades. As his parent, I do think you might want to listen to all the arguments your son has to offer about the wisdom of dropping a course. Often a faculty member will advise a student to drop his own course and take it when he might have less interference from the emotional toll of adjusting to college or a course load of several difficult subjects.

Your contributions

During high school it may have been a natural process for you to proofread, make suggestions or correct your son's papers. But you must now ask, "Why am I doing this?" If you are doing this because you think your son doesn't have the necessary skills to write a good college paper, this is important information. You want to refer him to a writing center on campus, where he can obtain a writing mentor. He may also be assigned a writing assistant with a first year course. This trained student will help him with papers for all writing assignments. It is important to help your son to transition away from your assistance with writing to the assistance of highly skilled professionals and paraprofessionals on the college campus. These helpers want to help him reflect upon his work and make this and the next paper better. It is not only inappropriate for you to assist your son with his work but also **if he turns in your writing as his own work it is plagiarism.** Students are expected to do their own work.

What simple memorable advice can you offer your son?

A is for attendance - Go to class

Now this sounds absurdly simple and obvious. But numerous students sleep through class or just choose not to go. Some of these students may experience anxiety about what might happen the next time they attend that class and therefore choose to skip it again and again and again. The student who gets caught up in this pattern is the exception, but he frequently does not make it beyond that first semester due to failing grades.

Many students who had good connections with teachers in high school are eventually able to translate this experience to their relationships with their college professors. The title of doctor or the size of the class intimidates others. Sometimes the relationship may be with a teaching assistant rather than the lecturing professor. It is important to establish a conversational relationship with the professor by visiting during posted office hours.

Once they have a working relationship, their continuing communication enhances and eases the academic experience. For example, the student who takes a draft in for feedback before it is due or informs a faculty member of an illness or emergency at home before the final hour will have the advantage in the classroom situation. There is nothing more frustrating to a faculty member than to have a deadline pass without student presence or explanation. My natural assumption in these situations is that the student is irresponsible and his negative attitude will be reflected in a lower grade. It is important for your son to talk to his professors not just to give excuses for lack of performance but also to find out more about them, their field, and the purpose of his learning. These early conversations can lead to a future mentor relationship. Your tuition dollar includes student-faculty interactions that will benefit your son academically and professionally. Encourage your son to take advantage of such opportunities.

Speaking of tuition dollars, my daughter tells me that at her expensive university, she and her classmates have figured out how much each class costs by dividing their semester tuition by the number of class hours. This cost analysis is frequently more jarring to the parent than a deterrent to class cutting by the student but it may be motivating if the student values the cost and recognizes the money wasted. Another source of motivation for attending class is the fact that when your daughter goes to class she is hearing the material that she has just read.

B is for Budget Studying

Prepare for Class

Studying on the budget plan yields the best retention of information. Studying a little every day will improve retention of information. Every student should read the assigned material before arriving in class. Reading means understanding, not just coloring in the pages with yellow, pink or green highlighters. One of my college classmates who graduated Phi Beta Kappa had an amazingly complex system of index cards with multiple colors organizing her textbook notes. This obviously worked well for her although I must admit that I was not someone who learned from her example. The ability to outline and reduce material to important essentials is invaluable. Perhaps you have prepared a report or speech for reading and outlining. Share your work with your son as a model he might want to consider.

Linda L. Bips, Ed.D. with Jessica and Kristina Wallitsch

Take notes in class

If your daughter reads the material before she goes to class, the teacher's lecture will be a review of the material. Remember A is for attendance? The student who doesn't go to class has missed one more opportunity to review and learn the material.

Rewrite notes after class

A third review ideally should take place within a day of class. This three-time rehearsal system puts the student in a good position for later review before an exam. Distributing rehearsals over time and including one more review before the exam allows for the "spacing effect," the best procedure for memorization. (Dempster,1988)

This form of studying is comparable to my gift closet. All year long I buy gifts that appeal to me or remind me of a dear individual. When the holiday season or a birthday comes, I go to my gift closet and take out the appropriate gift. When the exam date arrives, your daughter can pull the appropriate information from her mental closet with no last minute shopping. A regular routine of studying in the library or her room every day results in academic success.

Plan ahead

Students need to be cognizant of the long-term deadlines. If there is a paper due the Friday before Thanksgiving break, it is not advisable for your son to wait until the week before to start the paper by visiting the library to request articles for his paper. Articles not found in the home campus library but available by interlibrary loan could take several weeks to arrive. Ideally the student needs to take the long distance date and divide the task into short workable goals such as visiting the library for research articles early in the semester. On the other hand students also need to work in short spurts by looking at test dates and seeing what material will be included on the tests. He should approach his school day and assignments the way you manage your workday with scheduled time for classes and study. How do you organize your work projects? Share your organizational principles with your son.

Students also need to ask for help when they need it. Encourage your son to start by meeting the professor or teaching assistant for a particular course. Stopping by before there is a test or a paper due is a good way to prepare and make sure he is on the right track. Professors or their assistants also frequently hold reviews or cram sessions before an exam. Your son could benefit from this extra help. He might want to apply for a one on one tutor from the academic office on campus. He may be able to meet with a tutor on a regular basis to review material and prepare for tests. Often this is a free service. Trained upper class students who are accomplished in a subject often make the best teachers because they have only recently mastered the material themselves and are familiar with the early steps of learning. Your son should take his tests and papers to a professor's office hours to get more feedback on how he could improve in the future. Also academic centers offer individual assistance, particularly for students with cognitive disabilities.

G is for Grades

I would be remiss if I did not devote some conversation to the subject of grades. During a period of time when I was in private psychological practice, most of my high school clients were in battles with their parents about grades. The best way to look at this topic is to address the question of "Who owns the grades?" Some parents will immediately respond, "We pay the bill, we own the grades." If you believe this, you have already set up a power struggle with your student. You are asserting that you own the grades when you actually have no control. Your son determines his grades by his performance and to prove his power over the grades, he may respond to your demands by failing, the opposite of what you have insisted he do. In extreme cases, these are the students who take out their anger by getting the lowest grades possible. It really does take a certain kind of effort to get the D's and F's. What does your son hope to accomplish? He wants to make you angry and he is usually successful when he brings home a 1.0 grade point average (out of a possible 4.0).

It is important to remember that when you go to work one consequence of your working behavior is a paycheck with appropriate increases or decreases based on the quality of your performance. The student's paycheck is his grade, a direct result of his performance in the classroom.

Too many times parents call a professor angered by a low grade only to be surprised when the professor reports that John's paper was two weeks late or that Susie did not come to thirty percent of the class meetings. Most of the time your student's grade will accurately reflect their production and maximum ability to achieve in a particular discipline. Another major difference from high school to college is that effort doesn't always count. A student once wrote me an email. "I spoke to my friends and they said for the effort I put into your class I should have gotten a better grade." Her grade was based on the points she earned on a 500-point scale that included tests, papers, class participation and extra credit. She earned her grade. As one colleague says, "A C paper rewritten several times may still be a C paper if that is all the student is capable of producing."

But what about the high achiever - a student who must attain perfection?

I have always been a very self-motivated person, esteeming ambition and drive. My parents never put any pressure on me to be academically successful, yet earning good grades has always been extremely important to me. Neither of my parents can understand when I get upset over a B+, for example, "as long as you do your best," has always been their mantra. While many students long to

have such relaxed parents, I am sometimes frustrated that they do not understand how important my academic goals are to me.

Megan senior

The bottom line is to know your child. Initially I greeted Kristina's high school grades with cheers but I eventually learned to restrain my enthusiasm and approval and ask her opinion of the grades she had earned. I learned to trust her judgement of her performance rather than assume I knew the meaning of the grade. We all remember the "gut B" course in astronomy and the religion course in which we learned so much but only got a C.

Frequently the grades earned first semester may be lower than later semesters. There should be some allowance on your part for the socio-psychological adjustment that takes place as the student learns to live on his own and manage the new academic scene. I do recommend, however, that a parent seriously consider time out for very poor performance during the first year. The parents who pay the bill for succeeding semesters after their student earns D's and F's perplex me. The best consequences for students who are not successful is a semester off including a paid job and seeking help with their academic limitations, psychological health or simple lack of maturity. Second chances should only come after the student proves that he/she is going to make good use of another opportunity.

What if your son is not communicating with you about his grades? Before you call the college ask yourself, "Why am I making this phone call?" If you are worried that something is wrong based on something that your son said, it might be better to come and visit him and have a probing conversation about his initial communication. Ask him to show you some of the graded work with comments that he has received back from his professors. It is important for you to establish communication with your son. He may not call you as an assertion of his independence.

Secondly, it is important to ask yourself, "What is my goal?" Do you want him to improve his work? Will going behind his back to check his progress with a faculty member motivate him to work harder in the future? Before you make that phone call or send that email you want to ask yourself these important questions of why and what is my goal. Your answers to these questions should lead you back to better communication with your son.

Here are three rules as another way to convey the ABG's:

1. Go to class

2. Talk to your professor

3. Do your work

I would add a rule #4 to Mom's list. Don't be afraid to ask questions. If your son or daughter is having difficulty understanding various concepts, advise them to ask questions in class. Also their professor always will have designated times they will be in their office (office hours). As a freshman, I remember feeling intimidated by going to see professors during office hours. I often felt as if I would be disrupting their working time. However, I soon found that they wanted students to come and talk with them. By senior year there was rarely a week that I would not go to "visit" a professor during his or her office hours.

Also Rule #5 – Go to class for the purpose of enjoying learning. Too often during my college experience I would go to class for the sole purpose of gaining the information I needed to master for the upcoming exam especially in classes I did not particularly enjoy.

I found that if I went to a class for the pure sake of being interested in the topic, I would do much better academically and learn something in the process. The most wonderful thing in college is that the student is able to pick their own classes (besides the core requirements). My advice as a previous college student to parents is to encourage students to choose classes they are interested in so that they can go to class for the "purpose of learning." Jessica

I hate grades but I've been a slave to them. I've always tried to keep my GPA up and sometimes in order to do that I've had to sacrifice the quality of my education. To keep up with the work, I've sometimes skimmed books and I've worked harder on the graded assignments than the "learning" ones. This takes all the fun out of getting an A.

The most important thing is that your daughter or son enjoys learning. If they are curious, passionate, or dedicated to what they are learning in class, then good grades will follow. They might not be A's or B's but as long as they feel their perspectives widening and their knowledge growing, they will be happy. Too many people I know just trudge through college taking the classes they have to with little enjoyment. Some try to take the easiest classes to get near that golden 4.0. Talk to your daughter, if she has incorporated what she is learning into her life and her conversation then she is doing things well. However, I have known some kids that take advantage of their opportunities. Don't let your kids do this; they should understand that college is a privilege. If the situation is extreme, the school might not let them return the following semester. I've seen this happen to a few people and their parents kept sending them back and they eventually were asked to leave again. One person I knew was required to work part time to pay their own way through school until his grades improved.

After only a semester, his grades went up to B's and he was allowed to go back as a part time student. Kristina

Chapter 5   Choosing a Major – Passion or Poison

1. **Encourage your student to select a broad array of classes**
2. **Your student's interests don't have to be your interests**
3. **Allow your student the freedom to explore and grow**
4. **Remember a major does not necessarily a career make**
5. **Encourage your student to major in her passion**

As we go through life, our ideas about our lifework change. When I was in seventh grade. I wrote an essay on how I wanted to be a lawyer. When I was in high school my goal was definitely to be a helper of people. When I visited my future college, a psychology professor advised me that if I wanted to be a teacher, I should not waste my parents' money by going to a private liberal arts college but should attend a less expensive state teachers' college. I

81

gave up all ideas about being a teacher and majored in psychology but spent all my time on stage in the theater department. My desire to help people was diminished by the psychology major rat lab requirements. Fantasies and facts mark our early career exploration. Age 18 is not the end point but one shutter stop in a life long movie of one's career development. Although I did eventually become a psychologist, it was a long and twisty road. I am sure that many of my undergraduate psychology professors are surprised to see my career designation, psychologist and professor, in the alumni directory. I reached my career goal in spite of my college education. What is your career development progression? Straight, narrow and ascending or a crooked path like mine? Keep in mind the plusses and minuses of the path you took and now let's look at your student's path and perception.

What the students say

"My parents have always wanted me to be a doctor." "I want to be a dance major but my father says I won't be able to make a living." "I love philosophy but what can I do with it?" "If I am a psychology major, I have to go to graduate school to be able to get a job." "If I want to work in a business, I have to be a business major."

These are the statements I have heard from hundreds of students. My advice has always been for a student to major in that subject about which she is passionate. School can be hard enough without taking extended classes in subjects because mom, dad, an older brother, Uncle Jake, a high school physics teacher or the softball coach said so.

> When my father told me I was to be an international relations major, I chose philosophy. When he told me to at least work at something that would make me a lot of money, I chose social work. Everything was always a fight, I guess because fundamentally we are the same person - hardworking, competitive and well intentioned.
>
> Angelica graduate

What is higher education

Higher education is not meant to be job training but an opportunity to expand all areas of one's mind and explore the world's knowledge.

It is common for students entering college, choosing schools, or majors (and their parents) to assume there is a correct or even a "best choice" to make. When they are unsure of picking the correct one they often become anxious about making a mistake. Even if the students are not anxious their parents are. By taking part in this game – often a vanity game for parents and students alike – parents communicate to their children that there really is a big risk here if they choose incorrectly or unwisely.

Joseph Lowman, Ph.D.
University of North Carolina

A liberal arts education, in particular, provides the opportunity to understand the world and live a fulfilling life. At mid-life members of our generation are more likely to regret not taking the art history, the philosophy or the economics course during our undergraduate years than remember the courses we took to please someone else. "On the job" skills' training is a lifetime process.

When we take a closer look at the developmental level of an 18-year-old, especially in today's world of extended adolescence, it is hard to imagine that he would be prepared to or even need to make a life long career decision. The reality for your son is that he will most likely hold an average of five or more jobs before he retires. Higher education offers students of today the opportunity to become critical thinkers, effective writers and persuasive speakers. What are the everyday skills that you use? Where did you learn how to write a good informational report or give an influential public presentation? These are the goals of an undergraduate education. These skills will be used across a lifetime of multiple career and volunteer endeavors. It is critically important to allow your daughter the time to explore. The curriculum requirements will provide the framework for a comprehensive education.

Undeclared major

The initial designation of undeclared is not a failure in decision-making but a way of keeping the door open to multiple pathways. Following a college's diverse core curriculum in the first and second year can often introduce a student to a subject or field he might never have experienced before coming to college. It is very important to realize that we are all limited in our knowledge of careers and fields of study by the experiences of those around us, and your son's time at college allows exploration beyond the limitations of his eighteen years and of your life experiences.

> So I am Medieval Studies concentrator. "What is that?" everyone asks. I say, "Well, it's the historical, artistic and socio-religious analysis of a particularly momentous and exciting period in world history." "What will you do with it?" "DO with it," I say, "Don't worry, I'll figure it out later," and smile big.
>
> Kerin junior

Choosing a major

Many students change their major one or more times during their college career. Others students delay their choices until their upper-class years. Our college requires students to declare their major by the end of their sophomore year. Every year, however, I have a student advisee or two who are still undeclared entering their junior year. Of course waiting a long time to choose a major or changing one's major several times can delay graduation in order for the course requirements for the final major to be completed. In a recent reentry group after a semester at sea, several students discussed extending their college career by adding a second major in their senior year. Exploration today can lead to career satisfaction tomorrow.

Counseling at a college with a strong reputation for its premedical program, I repeatedly work with students who come to college on a single track. Their reasons are many. Money - parents, particularly non-professionals, may believe that becoming a doctor is the only way for their child to attain wealth and prestige and encourage their first generation college student to pursue a degree in one of the few fields they know anything about. Tradition - parents who are physicians may wish the family legacy to continue so the child emulates the parent. Love and/or ability in the sciences - lack of success in that first general chemistry course, an essential ingredient of any science major, sadly dismays students who loved high school biology. Whatever their motivation, a substantial percentage of students who enter college on a pre-medical track change direction at some point. In some ways the luckiest students are the ones who realize this is not the right direction in their first semester and have the rest of their college careers to explore a variety of majors. During his senior year, a student who had been accepted by several prestigious medical schools realized he had not had the opportunity for self-exploration. He acknowledged his doubts and other interests and initially deferred his acceptance at medical school. He never went. He is currently working in the social services as a helping professional and has not furthered his education. A more open door regarding majors and career path in the early years might have made for a more fulfilling undergraduate experience. Although initially disappointing to student and family, a change in major may be an important time for exploration and growth. A second semester freshman who left the premed track for a psychology major says,

My whole life I have wanted to be a doctor and my parents have also wanted me to be a doctor. It is very hard to change direction like that. But the most important thing is for parents to know that their kids will do what they want in the end. It's their life! Parents just need to be supportive and not excessively demanding and their kids will, in the end, make them proud.

Mark first year

Another first year premedical student had incredible artistic talent. She eventually majored in art and psychology and is currently seeking certification to teach art to elementary students. Another artistically talented student who was initially premedical combined her love of biology and art into a career as a medical illustrator.

Changing majors

Another reason for changing majors can be lack of success. If your son is not making the grades in the sciences, he may find that he can be more successful in theater or another field. Frequently a student enters a major with a particular goal, such as acting or directing but finds a future career in light design or producing children's theater, expanding the application of his education both in his major and other courses such as child development or entrepreneurship.

In a chat with my best friend and roommate this summer, she expressed her frustrations regarding continuing honors work within her chosen field or dropping the dreaded thesis and 'doing the dream' of theater that has always been hers. I concocted a suggestion in a sentence that she has written over her bed for inspiration and daily support. "Sometimes it is the stuff you find yourself doing when you are supposed to be doing something else that you really should be doing with your life."

Savina junior

Many students change their major one or more times during their college career.

A college major does not a career make. One can't, in other words, directly translate many majors into specific jobs. My younger daughter selected English as her major. Recently her university published an article on all the diverse careers English majors had entered including preaching, teaching and white water guiding.

Helping your student

Recommend that early on he take a broad array of introductory classes and electives. Ask him to follow up with conversations about careers with the faculty in subject areas of interest to him. Have her visit the career services on campus. Trained professionals are not just about job placement but are there to help your daughter from step one – determining her interests. Use your contacts to help your son locate an internship, a summer job or even an information interview with company's employees in his field of interest. But always keep the word "explore" in mind and make sure your efforts are about your daughter's interests and not what you think your daughter should be interested in. Whether your son shows an interest in the humanities, the social sciences or the sciences, you need to listen to his rationale and support his passion. Finally if he loves his subject, he has a much better chance of doing well. One of the major contributors to poor grades is disinterest.

Life is full of unknown dangers and opportunities. In effect, students make their choices good ones or bad ones; the outcome of a given choice doesn't exist before it is made. A school's perceived status or the opportunities for a given major or career path has no value in itself. It's what a student does at a school or in a major or career that matters most. Students need parents to help them come to realize this, something that is hard for students still at an earlier developmental stage in which they believe knowledge really exists as concrete facts rather than "explanations in progress." Parents can best help their children make such choices, whenever they come up before and during their college careers, by affirming that these decisions do not guarantee success and satisfaction nor failure. Communicate explicitly and implicitly that the decision made is not so crucial. It is what the student does with it and how chance or uncontrollable events play a part in the future that matters most. Emphasize to your child that the major is not the most important information on their diploma. Their own name and what kind of person they have become is what matters most.

Joseph Lowman, Ph.D.
University of North Carolina

There is always so much stress associated with choosing a major in college. As a college freshman, we do not know what we want to do with the rest of our lives. Therefore, when so much weight is put into figuring out a major, we get anxious about picking one that everyone else says is the right one.

It is better not to rush into choosing a major just to have one. I would encourage parents to guide their child into choosing a major that they feel passionate about. The core curriculum courses may spark a different interest, but in the mean time your child will enjoy going to classes, learning, and exploring a field that they feel excited about. Jessica

When choosing a major, it is important to keep the mind open. Students should take a wide variety of classes to try out different subjects. This will help them get a sense for the strengths of each department, some have good classes, some have good professors, and some are just a bunch of interesting books. Some majors are largely based around general requirements that may or may not be useful to an individual.

A good way to start this process is to visit an advisor. Usually a student will be assigned one as a freshman but this selection is not set in stone. I didn't realize this until my last year and I never looked forward to my meetings. When I had some trouble with credits, I went into the college office and met a wonderful woman who helped me straighten things out. For the last year I went to her whenever I needed help and things went much more smoothly. Your daughter deserves a competent and friendly person to go to for advice; it just may take a little bit to find the right fit.

It is good to think about a major early on in college. Not because there is any rush to make a decision, but it is helpful to be aware of requirements. What does the school require? What does the major require? These kinds of questions are good to keep in mind even in the earliest stages.

Before I went to college, I called a student advisor on the phone to get some advice about classes. She told me a wonderful piece of advice, "It is true that you want to take a well-rounded, diverse mixture of classes. But it is also very important that you come out of college feeling like there is some unity in all of the things that you have learned." This means different things to different people. Students should allow their interests and curiosity to guide their class selection. Kristina

Chapter 6   Cash or Credit

1. **Your student should contribute some portion of the college expenses**
2. **Help your student learn the skill of budgeting**
3. **Talk about who will pay for what**
4. **Have your student do a one month record of expenses**
5. **Open a checking account with a debit card**
6. **Educate your student about the cost of credit**
7. **No credit cards**
8. **Only take on campus employment**

Over the years working at a college, my coworkers are frequently neophyte professionals right out of graduate school. With a monthly paycheck to manage, one young staffer frequently bemoaned the fact that a week before payday she did not even have the funds to buy lunch. After listening to my speech to parents about budgeting, she heartily endorsed the idea of assisting your college age daughter in learning skills of budgeting. She had been one of the "lucky then sorry now" individuals whose parents had always picked up the slack for her spending beyond her means. She never learned the fine art of budgeting. Now at 24 she was in her first job and unable to make her paycheck stretch to the end of the monthly pay periods. Do your daughter a favor and help her learn the skills now. You can be a financial consultant to your daughter during this leaning period. Even if budgeting is something that your income doesn't require, there is no guarantee that your daughter will reach your economic success level.

Students today have all types of financial arrangements. Some "full payers" bring their parent's credit card tucked in with their college ID/key holder and spend without limits. At the other end of the spectrum are the students who have no parental financial support. Tuition bills are met through loans, work-study arrangements, and scholarships/grants offered through the college financial aid office. Students with financial aid may pay for other living expenses with some grants or earnings from extra jobs. And then there are the majority of students using some combination of parental, college and work funds. Good parenting fences include limits on the spending of Mom and Dad's money. All students should contribute to their college expenses.

> It is important to emphasize that your child spends his/her own money. By having a 9-5 job over the summer, at roughly 10 dollars an hour, your child can make enough to have for school. Not only is this instilling responsibility in the work place, but in their bank account. Most checking accounts come with books that let you record each expenditure or deposit. And some even send you a monthly statement. If this is followed - money management is easy. Encourage thinking ahead.
>
> Christina first year

Making a budget

It is very hard to estimate the day-to-day costs of college before your student gets there. You can estimate the big-ticket items like tuition and room and board from the college literature. Students may have their first month spending money wiped out with their first bookstore bill. Books can be very expensive, particularly when you buy brand new texts before classes begin. Frequently students can buy books from other students. Their professor might suggest students that would want to sell their books from the year before. Also faculty do change books and editors change editions so it's important for your daughter to go to class, get her syllabus and find out what she needs before she purchases the books.

Building a budget is something that we all have had to do whether at home or at work. Estimating the costs is a task best done by you and your daughter. Have her do some of the research by contacting an upper-class student or two who can give her an idea about all those miscellaneous categories. Remember to include phone, transportation at school and to and from school, clothing, entertainment, and also the miscellaneous like pizzas and sorority dues.

Who will pay for what

Now comes the most important conversation. A simple spreadsheet can be used. Start with the college and bank contributions and then deduct what you can afford and are willing to pay, and what is left is the responsibility of your son. Will his summer job cover the costs for one semester or the whole year? Will he need a winter break job to cushion the second semester? Will he need a job on campus or off campus? How many hours per week will he need to work to meet his expenses? This conversation is very important. Many parents are secretive about their finances and don't like to tell their son the where's and how's, but now is the time to open the doors to any financial information that will affect your son's ability to stay in school. Is his tuition dependent on you continuing in your current job? Are there a savings account, life insurance policy, a trust fund or an inheritance that are part of the assets? If your son knows the facts he will be better able to deal with problems along the way. This conversation is even more important in the case of divorced parents. Who will pay for what and how? Will mom and dad pay their tuition contribution separately or will one pay it all and collect the other's contribution. Put all the facts on the table as you assist your son in building his budget.

First month expenses

I suggest a dry run in September. Have your son itemize in his planner every item he spends a dime on, including that first shocking telephone bill. City, suburban or rural colleges require different finances. My younger daughter's initial budget was based on her sister's suburban school needs. The amount was insufficient for city life that often required such items as cab rides at night for safety. An initial one-month accounting excluding books provides an estimate of monthly expenses. At this time, parent and student can sit down again and readjust the figures by category and the sources. Your son can then start to live within his budget with appropriate readjustments based on continued documentation after several more months of school.

How do the bills get paid

There are various payment plans provided by the college for tuition and room and board that you and/or your daughter will want to investigate. If you plan to provide money for other budget items for your daughter you may want to divide up the annual or semester sum into monthly payments to match her budget figures. Also this is good preparation for the real world where most of us get paid at least once a month. This way she will be managing even though it is your money. A checking account is a good idea. Having one in your hometown allows you to deposit money but may make it difficult for her to cash checks. The debit card is a great way for her to be spending only the cash on hand. Many colleges have their own debit or flex systems that she can use for on campus incidentals, and again a monthly amount could be deposited to these accounts. A phone card is always a nice extra for calls home or for emergency calls when on the road. Speaking of emergencies, a credit card in your name only for emergencies may give you peace of mind that she won't be stranded on the highway without gas.

Credit cards

I recommend against a personal credit card account particularly for first year students. This population is a prime target for credit card companies. In 1998, 65% of the total collegiate population had personal credit cards. There is a time and place to learn to handle credit but it is not the first year of college - maybe not even the last year. Recently a counselor from an Ivy League college talked about several graduating seniors each with a debt of over $20,000. The average student balance on a credit card is over $2,100.

My personal finance rule is never charge something you can't pay off on that month's bill. I may use savings to pay it but I don't accrue credit card debt. Share information with your daughter about the $50 charge today and what it will cost in 7 years using the minimum payment model. It is also important to help your son understand how a few missed payments will impact his ability to borrow money for something important in his adult life or may even prevent him from obtaining a particular job when the company does a credit check.

Should your student work

Finally it is important to discuss the question of employment. There are usually jobs available on campus.

Some are only available to students who qualify for financial aid. These are called work-study jobs. Despite the name, every student knows the jobs where they can study, like sitting at the art gallery desk, and where they work, like delivering audio-visual equipment. After the first few weeks of school when the financial aid students have been employed, some of these jobs may open up to all students. There also may be other jobs available for any student on campus. The advantages to these jobs are location and the boss's realization that your son is first and foremost a student. Some students might find off campus employment appealing. It takes a good student to be able to balance college life with work. Twenty five percent of the entering college freshmen in 2001 were expecting to be employed full time, around 40 hours a week. I recommend against off campus employment during the first year if it is financially possible. Commuting home on weekends to maintain a job or working in town may interfere with adjustment and developing that critical sense of belonging. An on campus job can not only help your daughter better organize her time and contribute to her expenses, but with a job such as tutoring or serving as a residence advisor she will receive training and enhance her educational experience, social life and leadership skills. And remember an on campus employer knows that academics are your daughter's top priority.

Your child will value money more if they need to contribute in some way. It is very easy to spend money at college and I was not as frequently spending it when I was working for my spending money. Learning how to budget my money was a very valuable lesson I learned in college. Jessica

The way you deal with your child and money depends on how much you have. Some students get a full ride and all the allowance they need and other students do it all by themselves. I don't think either extreme is the right way to go.

I was lucky that my parents had planned to support me throughout my schooling, but it didn't stop me from working. I held various jobs around campus; working at a well-visited student bar was my first job. I had a great time working a few nights a week, socializing, meeting new people and getting paid as well.

In my sophomore year I worked for an international student center run by my university. There was much more responsibility involved but I enjoyed getting to know people from all different parts of the world. I also took off from paid employment some semesters to concentrate on my schoolwork. I found that I missed working, but sometimes a student needs to know when to just be a student.

I do strongly encourage every student to work during the summertime and get at least one internship before their college days end. Build the resume, test different career fields, otherwise heading into the real world after graduation could be a real shock. Kristina

Chapter 7 Roommates – The Art of Compromise

1. **Parents should not become involved in roommate disputes**
2. **Allow time for adjustment between the roommates**
3. **Don't call the residence life staff on behalf of your student**
4. **Know who your student can call and encourage him to use those resources**

I frequently ask incoming students to raise their hands if they have had to share a room with someone, usually a sibling, at some point in their lives. At our college, very few students raise their hands. I am reminded of the five months that my daughters and I found ourselves between houses living in a two-bedroom apartment and the ensuing battles between them as we tried to negotiate their sharing of a room. We eventually resorted to a line of masking tape down the middle of the room, a solution proposed in a storybook from their childhood. There was great relief for all three of us when our new home included a room for each of them. For Jessica and Kristina, these were the only five months of their lives until each went away to school during which they shared a room.

> I think that boundaries should be made from day one. We have roommate contracts that we always refer back to. They help with a lot of problems.
>
> My roommate calls us Martha Stewart (me) and Pig Pen (her). Having our room literally divided down the middle makes it easier because although she is messy, it is obviously on her side only.
>
> Lindsay first year

The importance of the roommate

Sometimes all of your son's expectations about college come down to whom his roommate will be. He may have high expectations of his roommate relationship, even believing that compatibility with his first year roommate predicts the success or failure of his entire college experience. It's important to assure your son that roommates are not forever, and that learning to live with another person is a yearlong process and a lifetime skill. After all, how many of you share your room with your spouse? Obviously most of you have learned the skill of cohabiting. Of course one difference is that in college this is your student's only space while you still have a house full of alternative spaces to call your own – your study, kitchen, sewing room, basement workshop and so on.

Parents stay out

The most important ingredient for a tolerable living situation anywhere is communication, and the most important ingredient for a tolerable living situation in college is for parents to stay out of that communication.

> Do not let your child become too dependent on you. Let them do things for themselves. It is difficult to deal with a roommate who is taking direct instructions from her mother.
> Allison first year

Some of the most difficult moving-in stories revolve around parents who have literally come to fisticuffs in the arrangement of the beds and dressers on the first day at college. Nothing could be worse for your daughter than for you to be in the middle of the two or more roommates making any arrangements. Hopefully you will do the basics of helping your daughter get her belongings into the room and then find something else to do so that she and her roommate(s) can begin to negotiate from day one what their room looks like and how they live.

One of my favorite stories was about the young woman who called home several days after move-in to ask her mother, "Where did you put my sweaters?" I often think of my houseguests who try to be helpful by putting things away and how long it takes me to find the plastic containers that they have put in the stove drawer that I reserve for pot lids. Your daughter's room needs to be arranged and organized by her. You can put things where she tells you as a helper in the process. Here's another point of view.

> Students should put their own things away so they know where they are. I, however, found it very helpful having our parents making suggestions and helping us move things about to find the perfect layout for our room.
>
> Katie first year

How to help

It is important to not intervene in the roommate relationship. If there is a problem among the roommates, you may find out to whom your son or daughter should go. Typically this will be someone in the residence life administrative structure starting with the resident advisor (RA), a student who may even live down the hall. If the intermediate steps don't resolve the problem, your son can contact the professional who runs the residence life and housing program. Have your son negotiate, communicate and make those contacts. This is his living situation. Will you be calling the landlord about his noisy neighbors when he is 28? I hope not, and now is the time to begin to allow him to figure out how to negotiate his living arrangements.

Compromises

A second semester freshman once described to me the art of roommate compromise. During the first few days of school, Kevin and his roommate often alternated being the last to bed at night. When Kevin was last to bed, he made sure all the shades were drawn down tight so as not to be awakened by the sunrise. When his roommate was last to hit the sack, he left all the blinds rolled up and the windows bare so the morning sun would awaken him. They didn't discuss this but realized that in the morning one would awaken to an unfamiliar light intensity in the room. When they finally realized what was happening and discussed it, they agreed to put the shades at the halfway point. Whenever I think about solutions to roommate problems, I picture the perfectly compromised shades in Kevin's freshman room.

> At the beginning of the year, my roommate always left for class when I was still sleeping, and she would leave the door wide open. It seemed like common sense to me to close the door like closing the blinds. Discussing it was what helped. Compromises help a lot. I need the TV to fall asleep and my roommate needs complete silence. We talked to our RA about it who suggested that we alternate TV on every other night. I think it is important to gain a feeling of trust with your RA because she will definitely help in a situation like that.
>
> Lindsay first year

Roommates come in all shapes, sizes and colors, with different values and habits. For eighteen years your daughter has been surrounded with people like her. This may be her first experience with someone who is a Hindu or

111

smokes or wears all black or stays up all night or reads her bible every evening or drinks or has sex with someone different every night in the bed above her. Some of this may sound shocking, but has it all really changed that much since the story of the sixties when the man left his tie on the doorknob to signal to his roommate not to enter and disturb his planned romantic activities for the evening? Think about how you have managed to get along with difficult people at work or in your extended family. Offer what has worked for you. Communication and compromise are the first two commandments of mutual living. It is also important to remember who owns the problem. This is her problem. Listen and advise but don't rescue or fix.

It is important for you to not physically intervene within the roommate situation and relationship, even if it is a negative one for your child. One of the best things you could do as a parent is just hear your kids out. Be that someone that they can vent to without further heating them up in regard to the situation at hand. No matter what, try and stay calm, and give them logical, rational advice even if what your child is telling you about what their roommate did or said angers you.

Lenore first year

Must a roommate be a best friend

Another important piece of advice that you can share with your student is that the best roommate is frequently not a best friend. First year students tend to make immediate, significant bonds with the people in closest proximity to them – roommate or hall mates. These friendships are frequently intense and ease the transition period from the familiarity of home to the loneliness of college. Nine times out of ten these friendships do not last beyond the first six weeks or what college administrators call the honeymoon period. Certainly there are life long friends who met as roommates the very first day of college, but they are the exception, not the norm. The happiest roommates are students who establish separate groups of friends and separate lives but like each other and respect each other in the room. If your son hasn't learned to be respectful of others in your own home, living with a roommate will be very difficult for him. Living with a roommate means being quiet late at night or early in the morning when your roommate may not have to go to bed or get up. It means keeping the room at a temperature that pleases everybody, which may mean putting on extra sweatshirts or walking around in your underwear. It means tolerating those differences, which after all is one of the important aspects of development at this stage of your son's life.

> I have three roommates and have formed different relationships with all of them. They have to create different relationships among each other as well. Roommates can be the greatest part of the college experience whether or not they are your best friends. The most important thing you can learn from a roommate is how to compromise and learn that selfishness will not be accepted in college.
>
> Rebecca first year

As a college freshman, I remember being very anxious about whom my roommate was going to be. I frequently asked myself questions such as, "Will I like her?" "Will she like me?" "Will she be like my friends from home?" I felt very lucky to find my roommate very easy to get along with. We had some similarities and also some differences.

Since she came to school two weeks early to play field hockey and attend a pre-orientation program, she already had her own group of friends. At first it was difficult to come to the realization that we weren't going to spend every minute together and be best friends (a misconception most freshmen have). This also forced me to make my own friends, a positive thing.

As roommates we communicated well and respected each other, trying to give each other space (which wasn't always easy in a small college dorm room). As the year progressed we got to be very close and our times together were some of my fondest memories of my freshmen year.

One of the activities our Resident Advisor had us do on the first day was write down our likes and dislikes and what we expected our roommate to do and not do.

When I transferred to another school after freshman year, I considered myself lucky again to have another wonderful roommate. We were both transfers, which made the transition for both of us easier. We became friends but also had our own sets of friends. We pledged different sororities and often went to separate social events. We enjoyed being together and hearing one another's stories, but were not together all the time. We had a very healthy roommate relationship.

On the other extreme was the semester I spent abroad. My roommate situation during that time was completely different. I spent second semester of my junior year on a program called Semester at Sea. Six hundred students traveled to places all over the world for 100 days. Being the least expensive option, I chose a triple on the ship sharing a room about the size of my previous double with two other girls. I remember calling my mother from the first port of call, "My luck with roommates just ran out." One of my roommates stayed up all night drinking, while the other one wanted our room totally quiet by 8:00pm so that she could get a good night's rest. I was stuck between these two extremes and often was put in the middle of the frequent arguments. Also limited to the ship's environs at sea, there weren't many places for me to go. This difficult situation taught me how important good communication between roommates is. Also you should always discuss feelings and expectations in the very beginning. I would advise parents to encourage their child to communicate and not be too upset if she does not like her roommate. Jessica

I've had all sorts of roommates, best friends, enemies, and somewhere in between. The best thing I've learned from my experiences is to start out on the right foot. You should encourage your son or daughter to have an honest and frank conversation with his/her new roommate.

You can help them get ready for this conversation. Ask your child about her lifestyle? What kind of things she needs in her environment? For example, does she need music or quiet when she studies? What does she find difficult about living with others? What might others find difficult about her? She should have a clear but flexible picture of the situation she is looking for.

It took me a while to do things this way. I'm not a confrontational person, but now I know that I'll be unhappy if I don't lay down the line and ask my roommate to do the same. The trick is to have the conversation when the two are first meeting, things are fresh and the roommates are optimistic about being friends and things tend to go smoothly. Kristina

Chapter 8   Managing Loneliness - It is Real

1. **Be patient with each other and with her loneliness**
2. **Provide long distance support and love**
3. **Have your student stay at school**
4. **Share times when you have been lonely**
5. **Provide coping strategies**
6. **Reassure her**

Every year when I address the parents of incoming students in June preceding freshmen year, I adapt an exercise from Coburn and Treeger's book *Letting Go*. I ask for volunteers. "Is any one willing to pack what you own, limited by the size of your car trunk and roof, and say good-bye to your spouse, children, community, pets and everything you know and love? When you arrive at this new place, you will be assigned to a room where you will live with one or more roommates. You will be starting a new job, which is similar to the job you have been doing in the past, but it will be more difficult. Everything will be new although you may have visited once or twice before. Volunteers?" When I finish this description the room falls silent although usually there are one or two brave souls that think it would be great to trade in their life at this point. These are usually folks persuaded by their middle-age status.

Going somewhere new and starting over with no support from your past is not something that any of us elect to do. Yet we ask our student to do just that. I shared this example with first year faculty advisors at a recent training workshop. One of the math professors later came up to me and stated that he had never really thought about the kind of adjustment we are expecting of the typical 18-year-old college freshman. He was now able to put his students into a context beyond just occupying seats in Calculus I. This is more than likely the most difficult transition period in one's life. It is important for parents to also remember this context. Would you volunteer? Really?

How do you cope with loneliness

The loneliness is real. When we end a love affair or move to a new place, we experience loneliness. Many of us want to immediately engage in a new love affair or make instant best friends. These are often also the solutions arrived at by new college students. They attempt to quickly establish intense relationships with new individuals to fill the space or void in their hearts left by the absence of a significant other, their parents and siblings, and those life long high-school classmates. Something that is often forgotten is that these previous long-term relationships became intimate by sharing experiences, emotions, and values over time. In the first encounters of freshman year, many students attempt to rush a process that cannot be rushed. It takes time to know another person. First impressions may not be trustworthy. An individual who is at first appealing and seems compatible may not be the person he initially presents. Also your daughter herself may change in her first few months at a new place into someone slightly different than the person who arrived in September, thus changing any new relationships. Some students use college as an opportunity to be what they never could have been before. Shy students report becoming more outgoing and gregarious. These are positive growth experiences but may result in conflicts in relationships that were established early on in the college experience. Your daughter may have a new best friend that becomes her worst nightmare by fall break. Those that hoped for life long college friendships may not find such companions until later - second semester, sophomore year or even beyond. If your daughter does find the love of her life only to leave him by Thanksgiving, understand her need to have some security during this stressful time. You both need to practice patience with each other and with her loneliness.

One of my floor mates and I had a deep and touching conversation the one night. We were discussing how hard it is to make close friends. You were probably friends with your friends from home for at least five or more years. As for the friends you make in college, how do you catch them up on the past eighteen years of your life so you feel like they know you and are close? We came to the conclusion that like everything else, it was going to take time and patience. Even if you can't be close right away, be sure to make friends. They will make you feel at home and most of all help to heal your loneliness.

Lindsey first year

Is it homesickness

Sometimes loneliness is homesickness. A student may be pining away for home, meaning friends and loved ones. It is very important to not immediately give in and bring your daughter home. Once she has reentered your world and reconnected with her old friends, even for a weekend, it makes it even more difficult for her to return to college. Students away for the weekend miss out on much of the informal campus life. This is the time when friendships are formed and common experiences occur. It may be a difficult time, and it may seem easier to go home to the local high school football game with old friends and to church with mom and dad. Time at home interferes with the college transition and a good adjustment.

I feel like there is a critical time period in the first month of your freshman year that you really have to be out there making friends. It is sort of weird, but after that time period it shuts down. It doesn't really open up again until the end of freshman year or the beginning of sophomore year. I missed that critical period. I went home, I was studying, and when I came back I would feel like I didn't have those critical social contacts. I didn't even know it was happening. I didn't feel like I belonged meaning this isn't the right place for me. I took it all

out on the school. I wonder how many of my other friends
were unhappy too.

Gwen senior

I recommend that students not return home until the first
official break, which is usually some time in October. Of
course there are exceptions like a sister's wedding or a
brother's Bar Mitzvah but even then keep the visit to the
official purpose. If you are not too far away and your
daughter continues to be homesick, make a visit to campus.
Have a meal; go to a campus event and leave. This will
keep your daughter on campus yet ease her need to see
someone familiar and close. Include one of her new friends
in some of the activity. Encourage your daughter to join
activities and get to classes. Being active and eventually
involved is the best way to put down those new tentative
roots. Meeting people around a common interest or class is
easier than trying to come up with small talk with strangers.

When will the lifelong friendships happen

I often advise first year students based on the
experiences upper class students share with me and on my

own experiences. Frequently one does not establish those long-term relationships until later in one's college career. One of my best friends was a woman who transferred into my college in the fall of my junior year. This two-year experience has been more significant to me lifelong than many of the early friendships of freshmen year. Some of my first friends were walking on the wild side, which appealed to me as I tried to adjust to the college environment. Then I adopted a group of goody two-shoe friends who didn't suit me and rejected me for my association with the less conservative group. I finally settled into a social group that seemed to fit my needs, matched my newly redefined values and some who shared my interest in theater on our campus.

How to cope with disappointments and difficulties

One of the observations that my colleagues and I have made in the past few years is that students are much less willing to experience discomfort, negative feelings or disappointments than the students of earlier generations. As adults we know that life includes failures, setbacks and

Find the relief you need.
And some peace of mind to go with it.

**Send this card in today to get your FREE
Understanding Pain Relief package.**

Visit www.understandingpainrelief.com or call 1-866-337-0900 now.

moisten, fold and seal

Pfizer respects your right to have your personal and health information kept private. We may use this information to send you materials on our products and services that may be of interest to you. Pfizer and the companies that work with us to provide these materials will not share your information with any other third parties or outside mailing lists.

☐ Along with the material you asked us to send, Pfizer may want to contact you from time to time about special offers and updates on arthritis, and related health issues. Check here if you would like this information.

☐ Check here if you also agree that Pfizer and companies working with Pfizer may use your information to help develop Pfizer products, services, and programs, provide you with materials you may find useful, and contact you about health-related topics.

If you do not check either box and don't sign below, we will fill just this one-time request.

Signature _____ Date _____

Name _____

Address _____

City _____ State _____ ZIP _____

Phone (optional) _____

E-mail (optional) _____

Have you been told by your doctor that your joint pain or arthritis is caused by one of the following?
(Optional: please check all that apply)

☐ Osteoarthritis
☐ Adult rheumatoid arthritis
☐ Other arthritis
☐ Have not been diagnosed by a doctor

Do you currently take any of the following for your condition?
(Optional: please check all that apply)

☐ Nonprescription or over-the-counter medicines
☐ Prescription medicine

If you take a prescription medicine for your condition, please write the name of it here: _____

compromises. One can well imagine how the combination of intolerance for discomfort and the loneliness of the beginning college experience can result in some difficult problems and inappropriate liaisons. This is when it is important in your role as a parent to provide the long distance support and love that your daughter has counted on since early childhood. Share your similar life experiences and how you handled the emotionally difficult separations and periods of loneliness. Reassure her that eventually she will connect with friends and loved ones that will become intimate and significant in her life.

I have been talking to my mother about my problems and feelings. She mentioned to me that perhaps the reason why I am not enjoying it, socially, as much as I would like to is because I am not opening up to people in a way that allows them to open up to me. I am not accepting people to be friends with me because they might not fit the mold of the friends I ave grown up with back at home. I thought that this was an interesting point, further proving my belief that mothers truly are right almost all of the time.

Marc first year

My younger daughter frequently describes my current role in mothering as the soother- the person who consoles and calms her. She knows and counts on my ability to say

125

the right thing and reassure her when she is feeling that things are beyond her control. I like the thought that I am a person that she can return to lifelong for that kind of comfort and succor and then move back into her emerging adult life.

The one she left behind

When I asked students to respond to my book, this topic received the most feedback from first year women. This is one of the first topics they discuss with each other. This is also one of the difficult problems for parents, feeling like they have no control.

Your daughter is leaving for school and she has a boyfriend at home. He may still be in high school or at home working or attending community college or off to another institution somewhere else. The strain of being separated from all loved ones plays a role in the your daughter's desire to maintain this relationship as a link to the familiar in a strange, new world. The couple's worlds soon become very different. The boyfriend who is still attending the high school football games and pep rallies has different interests than the young woman who is now studying philosophy and/or going to fraternity parties every Friday and Saturday night. As a parent you may be anxious for this relationship to end. Either you have always disliked this young man or you worry that the relationship will interfere with your daughter's full appreciation of her college experience. As you probably already know your daughter's investment in a partner may escalate in direct proportion to your disapproval.

One year during orientation, a male student arrived at his first advising group meeting with his high school girlfriend in tow. She sat through the first day of activities requiring her boyfriend's constant attention and not only distracting from his experience but also interfering with the advising group activities. His student advisors sought help from the administrator in charge who had a chat with this student. His girlfriend then returned to his parents' hotel room. On the next day of orientation, he attended no activities so he could spend the day with her.

I remember sitting with first year women during an orientation dinner as they compared notes about their high school boyfriends. One of them said how angry it made her when anybody predicted the imminent and inevitable end of her relationship now that she was off to college. The others at the table agreed that they would prove the nay sayers wrong. Need I add the that the nay sayers were right but your saying nay will only complicate the process and antagonize your daughter.

A local student once came to campus with her high school boy friend who never left her side. She had limited her college choices to schools near her home in order to stay close to him. She had decided to live at home and commute so she could spend all her free time with him. She was now battling with her parents about living at school. Her father consulted with me because he was concerned that Karen would be missing out on college if she continued this relationship. He decided to insist that she live on campus for the first semester and explained his desire for her to take full advantage of college life. She came to college, moved into her room and within a week she had ended the relationship with her hometown boyfriend. Now the parents were smart because they did not insist that she end the relationship, only that she live on campus. Most problem situations aren't so easily resolved. I remember another student with a similar scenario who moved onto campus and immediately disappeared from her room. She took advantage of not being under her parents' watchful eyes to stay out night after night with her local boyfriend. By midterms she was failing all her courses and had to leave the college. I have known students who went to their hometown to visit friends and, to circumvent their parents' wishes for them to stay at school, stayed with friends. The parents never knew their daughter was down the street instead of at college.

One way to discourage your daughter from coming home is to enforce the rule of no cars for first year students. Also encourage your daughter to become involved in activities on campus. It can be really uncomfortable to go to the high school senior prom when you are a second semester freshman in college. Finally I wanted to share some of the many responses to this problem that I received from first year college women.

When I arrived at college I had the same syndrome. I believed that my boyfriend and I would stay together forever. It lasted only two months before I ended it. Give your child time and let them make their own decisions. Students need to stand up for themselves, and if they want to have fun at school and enjoy their college experience don't let their boyfriends at home control them.

Stephanie first year

And an opposite point of view.

Long distance relationships can work if you choose to make them work. My boyfriend is a senior in high school yet as a freshman in college I have found no other person here who even somewhat rivals him. In addition to being very much in love, we are also best friends. We send email twice a day, plan time for phone calls, and even occasionally have visits on weekends. However, this has not killed my social life nor has it jeopardized my grades. There are many people who will tempt you or advise you against a long-distance relationship. However, you should never compromise what you feel in your heart to be right.

Jerzy first year

Throughout my college search my parents disapproved of my serious relationship with my boyfriend, insisting that no matter what I did or where I attended school I would not be happy without my boyfriend. This made me angry and caused many fights between my mother and I; however, my boyfriend remained the stabilizing factor throughout it all.

My mother wanted me to attend a college closer to home, and she didn't think I would be happy being four hours away from my boyfriend. Although I took this into consideration the fact that she was using it against me made me very angry.

My parents insisted, "If all you care about is staying with your high school boyfriend then you should just go to a college in our hometown." Granted, they just said this sarcastically in hopes that it would make me break off the relationship. Throughout the entire time my boyfriend insisted that nothing should make me go anywhere I didn't want to and that I shouldn't make any decisions because of our relationship – he maintained that whatever happens, happens and all that matters is that I go to the school I want.

My high school boyfriend was the stabilizing factor that ultimately helped me realize that the most important thing in my life right now is I. He convinced me that even he shouldn't have such a great influence on my life as to determine my college choice.

With one semester complete and the second off to a great start, I see that it is possible to maintain a high school relationship while also having a great college experience. Although I agree that high school relationships can definitely be detrimental to one's college career this was not the case for me. Parents should let their children try to work though their relationships by themselves before they reprimand or try to terminate them. Chances are they will eventually make the right decision. I know that all my parents really wanted was for me to make my college decisions based only on what I wanted for myself, not my relationship. I did this and everything has worked out great.

Keveney first year

And the last word.

I found myself in this position my senior year of high school, and I am currently trying to maintain a relationship with my boyfriend this year. My mom never insisted on our relationship ending, but she did make it a point that I open myself up to every single college experience. During my first semester here I was constantly arguing with my boyfriend about my new college life. I love being in the relationship but if I had one piece of advice for college freshmen pertaining to relationships it would have to be leave him or her behind – move on, experience college at its best and if one day you meet up again that is wonderful – otherwise you will be missing out on so much that you might not even realize you've missed until it is gone.

Julie first year

131

It is somehow strange to think that a college student surrounded by perhaps thousands of other college students, stimulated by an exciting new environment, can feel lonely. It is, however, the transition from being comfortable at home with family and friends that know you well, to coming to a completely new place that can make the freshman college student feel lonely or homesick.

For me, the first few weeks were difficult - adjusting to being away from my friends and family. Others may take a few weeks, months, or perhaps a full year. For some of my friends loneliness was never an issue. The thing that worked best for me was thinking of things that would keep me busy and happy. I always felt better after working out at the gym. This soon became a part of my daily routine. I also joined many of the campus clubs. This kept me busy as well as developing a sense of accomplishment.

Also when I would be missing home sometimes, it was better not to call and I tried to rarely go home for the first few months as a freshman. If I were really missing my family, they would come to visit me. This is a good strategy for parents to consider. If you are close enough to your son or daughter go visit for an afternoon if they are homesick, do not encourage them to come home. It is better if they stay and try to make the adjustment.

I found that many of my friends who went home every weekend would miss out on so much and had a more difficult time adjusting to college life.

Encourage your son or daughter to get involved, do activities that they enjoy and most importantly STAY AT SCHOOL. Jessica

Mid-way through my freshman year, the loneliness hit. The first months had been so easy for me that I thought it never would. I was wrong. I went through a cycle that is familiar to many students. I made friends fast and furiously and felt like the friendships would last forever. We did everything together and in big groups. Then one day the schoolwork started to kick in and the social scene calmed down. I found myself feeling alone, and my friendships felt artificial. On top of all this, my roommate and I were having our first argument.

I remember going out into the hallway and calling my mom. I hadn't talked to her for a while, and she could tell I was upset right away. I couldn't explain it all, so I concentrated on my most recent woe. Most of my friends were pledging a frat or sorority and even though I knew Greek life wasn't for me, I felt excluded because it was taking up all their time. As I went on and on, she listened and sympathized. When I was done complaining I felt a load was taken off my shoulders. I was ready for suggestions and she had lots of them. Did I want her to plan a trip to visit me? What about my friends who weren't pledging? Was I still thinking about going out for sailing? These questions forced me to look at the optimistic side of things, and since I had just spent a half hour complaining, I was ready to be cheered up.

Everything worked out for the best. I soon realized everyone was going through the same thing. Friendships shifted and then settled down again. My mom had helped me look at the big picture rather than concentrate on the little things. And in the meantime, I worked on making things better. I joined the sailing team. I met friends that weren't pledging and made sure to keep in touch with the ones that were. By the time the dust settled, my relationships had taken on a depth and permanence for which I had been longing. Kristina

Chapter 9 College Landmines

<u>Eating</u>

1. **Teach and model healthy eating**
2. **Make sure your student has access to healthy food**
3. **Don't make casual comments on your student's gain or loss of weight**
4. **Mandate an evaluation if there are trouble signs**

One of the largest challenges for college students, particularly women, is the trap of eating disorders. At my college in the 1960's, there was a student down the hall who ate nothing but blew up like a blimp and left school by Thanksgiving. A woman next door started taking diet pills, prescribed by her family doctor, and eventually starved herself to an unhealthy weight and left school. A young sorority woman told all her friends about her new method of losing weight - vomiting after an evening of beer and pizza, thus negating the calories. No one called these problems anorexia, starving oneself, or bulimia, bingeing and purging, but disordered eating has always existed on the college campus. Many young women come to college today having experienced bulimia for years or being veterans of treatment for anorexia nervosa while still in high school. Unfortunately, these diseases of adolescence have spread down into the middle school and high school populations. Since eating disorders affect 98% women and only about 2% men, I will address the majority of my comments to the parents of daughters.

Whether your daughter is eating too much or too little or the wrong food is a concern for every parent. I remember my daughter's report of a high school summer cheerleading camp where her friends did not eat breakfast or lunch. Frequently Jessica had to beg someone to accompany her to dinner where her friend would eat as little as possible. Meanwhile the girls were participating in four very physical training sessions per day. Her friends spent many hours talking about losing weight and ideal bodies. The number of female students who report very disturbed and disordered eating patterns dismays me, and yet their behavior would not fit the strict criteria of anorexia or bulimia. How does a parent begin to deal with the problem of a daughter's disordered/problem eating?

Teaching and modeling

Teaching proper nutrition to our daughters starts very early on. It means having healthy food in the house from the time that they are toddlers. It is important to set a good example for your daughter in the way that you eat and to offer nutritional advice in an indirect way. I have found in trying to directly confront my concerns about my daughter's eating that I am met with resistance and denial. Modeling and some educating are the best tools for early prevention. I share such facts as the importance of eating something in the morning to not only provide fuel for the brain so that studying is productive but also the opportunity to give one's metabolism a kick start to functioning for the entire day.

Food access

It's important to make sure that your daughter or son has access to proper food. The majority of colleges offer food plans and many require them for first year students. The cooking is not mom's, and institutional food does get boring although today there are stir fry stations, salad bars, frozen yogurt machines, etc. When my younger daughter attended a city school, I encouraged her to sign up for a food plan anticipating that it would be difficult for her to meet her nutritional needs without cooking facilities. After just a few weeks on this food plan, she switched to a five meal a week plan and a special card with flexible finances available so that she could take advantage of the many other food opportunities surrounding the college campus. It was important for me to listen to her needs and respond to the setting that she found herself in. It is important to make sure that our students also have enough proper food in their room. It is very difficult to maintain fruits and vegetables even with a refrigerator. I know as a single person living alone, the bag of lettuce gets brown quickly. Although homemade chocolate chip cookies may be the care package of choice, it's always a good idea to also provide nutritional breakfast bars and other dried storage foods that can provide your student with some good nutrition.

"The freshman 15"

Students who eat in an unhealthy way the first semester at college are said to gain 15 pounds. The slogan has been around since before I went to college and continues to apply. Eating can include the midnight pizzas, cafeteria-style smorgasbord and beer. The weight gain can also be accelerated by the discontinuance of high school athletics or regular exercise. Women find themselves going home for winter break, unable to fit into their clothes. Some of these women begin to eat more healthily and start to incorporate exercise into their life. A few of these women in their attempts to reclaim their former figure try binge diets, vomiting, or excessive laxative use which can lead to anorexia, bulimia or other disordered eating patterns. Long-term experience has shown us that bulimia does not control weight. Bulimic students tend to actually be on the heavier side and do not attain their stated dieting goals by purging but rather suffer many serious consequences of the purging behavior including physical problems like loss of tooth enamel, irritation of the esophagus, stomach problems, etc.

Sometimes a weight loss garners compliments from classmates that reinforce the disordered eating. These women can often be found on the treadmills for hours at a time. All they can think about and frequently talk about is the food they are or aren't eating. Too many times a student will describe their eating for the day to include a half of a bagel for lunch and lettuce and a small amount of pasta for dinner. I remember the student who told me she eliminated her lunch bagel because of its fat and calorie count and replaced it with a hot pretzel. These women know calories and fat content better than they know their history facts for tomorrow's exam. Even with minimal knowledge about nutrition, we know that this routine provides insufficient calorie intake and that their bodies' metabolism will slow down to counteract the limited intake. A symptom of an eating disorder is an inaccurate body image. One student told me that she went shopping for jeans and the size 2 fell off her hips. In the same session she complained about her fat thighs. In extreme cases these women become too ill to continue in college.

Family response

The summer after that first year can be a fertile field for disordered eating. Seemingly harmless remarks by well-meaning family or friends about weight gain can trigger dieting and exercise. The trouble comes when the behaviors become compulsive and the thoughts about food and appearance become obsessive. Although frequently we see a change in our student's appearance, we attempt to reassure ourselves by their behavior when they are home. Students tell me that they eat to meet their parent's expectations while they're home but immediately revert to their habits of starvation and purging upon returning to school. Home behavior, therefore, is not a good indicator.

A hallmark of disease is secrecy which makes intervention by college officials or family even more difficult. Students do not take kindly to the advice or knowledge of parents. Frequently, parents need to intervene and take control of the situation in order to save their daughter's life. If your daughter or son is showing an increasing loss of weight, it is important to have them examined by your family doctor to make sure that their health is not being affected. Although throughout this book I recommend a parenting approach with proper privacy boundaries, when a student is in trouble those boundaries need to be put aside. You should mandate that a professional evaluate your daughter if you see signs of trouble like sudden weight change, cessation of menstrual cycles, different eating patterns and excessive exercise.

This is not a text on eating disorders. The most important thing to know if your daughter shows signs of disordered eating is to get three professionals involved – a physician, a nutritionist and a therapist.

I knew many people in college with eating disorders. They were struggling with gaining weight as a result of a new lifestyle as well as the desire to look thin. I kept healthy in college by exercising regularly and by eating 3 meals a day. Many students skip meals and feel that they are too busy and stressed to exercise. I found that eating healthy and working out helped to reduce my stress and build my self- confidence. As a parent, you will not be able to control your child's eating habits. It is best to encourage them to exercise and eat healthy. Instead of sending care packages full of sweets, send them fruit and healthy snacks. Also, watch for warning signs of an eating disorder. If you see any signs of eating disorders it is important to get your child help right away. Jessica

Stress/Anxiety

1. **Pay attention to stress signals in your student**
2. **Share techniques that reduce stress for you**
3. **Talk over your student's perceived pressures**
4. **Demonstrate the skill of prioritizing**
5. **Accept imperfection in your student, and yourself**

Many a parent may ask in disbelief, "How can college life be stressful?" It seems like the ideal life to those of us who worry about meals and mortgages, work and family. There is your son living in a nice residence hall with a bed, desk and closet, bathrooms and laundry down the hall, and a full buffet at every mealtime resembling the local mall food court. He has minimal cleaning and cooking responsibilities. His room includes all the modern entertainment and communication devices to keep him in touch with his college and outside world. He is expected to attend class only about 15 hours per week. When he has outside academic work, he has his choice of study environment and the services of the Internet in addition to the more traditional library services of reference materials, research indexes, interlibrary loan and even free loans of the latest DVD's. Usually, a fully equipped recreational center is within walking distance including a weight room, swimming pool, basketball court, squash and tennis courts and an array of exercise machines that rival any fancy health club. He additionally has a wide variety of on campus entertainment to choose from including first run movies, campus comedians and musicians, plays and concerts, and an eveready social group for partying or just hanging out 24-7 (as in hours in the day and days in the week). So what is there to be stressed about? Just about everything.

Stressed students of today

In a survey of first year students in 1999 by the Higher Education Research Institute at UCLA's Graduate School of Education & Information Studies about 30% of the freshmen felt overwhelmed by all that they had to do. In the 2001 survey of entering college freshmen only slightly more than 50% rated their physical and emotional health in the highest 10%. This was a record low percentage. And for women the percentage fell below 50%. The numbers confirm the impression of higher education administrators and faculty that students are more stressed. And these numbers are prior to the terrorism of September 11, 2001.

Good stress – bad stress

Research shows us that a little stress can be a good thing and often moves us toward optimal performance. Sometimes the excitement of new places, new people and academic competition can cause the adrenaline to pump and energy to flow. When one or more areas of your daughter's life become stressful, she may enter a subsequent stage of stress – resistance. Eventually she may experience exhaustion or burn out. Once exhausted she becomes non productive and vulnerable to depression.

Why are students stressed

The transition from being dependent on your parents to being independent is one of the most if not the most stressful period in psychological development. In addition to the developmental stress, your son exists in an academic and social pressure cooker. Your son is anxious to be accepted by his peers, make friends and make the grade in the classroom and perhaps also on the athletic field. Change is more stressful for some individuals than for others but there is no one who doesn't experience some stress during transitional life stages.

The source of his stress can also be excess pressure or demands from just one area of his life such as difficult academic expectations and less than desired performance. The combination of academic requirements - readings, writings and test taking, and social pressures - a broken relationship and leadership responsibilities - organizing an event and pressure from you can reach a level resulting in overload on the stress meter.

Signs of stress

When we experience a high level of stress, the body begins to break down. Signs of stress in students include the inability to sleep, eating too much or too little, or worrying to an excessive degree about insignificant matters. As the student becomes more stressed, she might experience anxiety. For example, students who may literally study too much and become so anxious about performing well on a test may experience test anxiety. The anxiety interferes with their ability to recall any information, resulting in the infamous "blanking out." In cases of test anxiety, I recommend that the student try one of several relaxation techniques. These techniques can be generalized to many other forms of anxiety.

Consulting for stress relief

As your daughter's consultant, you want to first consider techniques that help reduce stress for you. We all have some form of stress in our work day or home life and most of us have developed ways of destressing – positive behaviors like the 5am run in the park or negative behaviors like the 5pm martini. Do you exercise, listen to music, talk to a friend or therapist, cook or clean, or practice deep breathing or muscle relaxing exercises for an immediate reduction in stress levels? These work because when your body is physically relaxed it cannot simultaneously be in an anxious state. So if you are able to mentally and physically bring your body to the point of relaxation, you will no longer be able to be anxious. If you have methods that work for you, please share them with your daughter. Students frequently use exercise to relax and this has many benefits beyond the immediate reduction of stress. Students who exercise also eat and sleep better and are better able to concentrate on their studies. It is great to lift weights, run around the track or swim a mile or two. Physical exercise is always a good way to combat stress.

I find that even during my most hectic and crazy weeks at college (3 tests, work, meetings, papers, etc), I always find time to take a run or play basketball. When I do this it allows my brain to have a break and it is enjoyable. My mom would always make sure that I took time to enjoy myself at college. She knows that I am a very hard worker, and that I put enough stress/pressure on myself. Knowing that she encouraged me to go out on the weekends helped me to realize that I could relax. She listens to my concerns and allows me to vent.

Becky sophomore

Another way of dealing with stress is to talk over the pressures with people who will listen. Since you are now practicing good listening skills, you can help reduce the stress of two exams in the same day and the infidelity of her boyfriend in your daughter's life by giving her a listening ear and a shoulder to cry on. Sometimes students deal with stress by using and abusing alcohol and drugs. Your after work cocktail may be your son's nightly 6-pack in front of the tube. These are not good ways to reduce stress. In addition to a temporary distraction, the longer-term consequences of such behavior continue to interfere with the ability of your son to focus on his studies.

Sometimes the impact of stress brings your son to the health center on campus with multiple physical symptoms. Not unlike your ulcer or chronic headaches, your son's physical maladies may have no physical basis. Up to 30% of the illnesses reported to college health centers are psychosomatic and are better cured by relaxation than medications. Stress is elevated at certain times of year, particularly when tests and papers are due at mid term and the end of the semester. The pressures of family situations that are argumentative or dysfunctional may add to a student's stress. Students often become very relaxed and comfortable in their campus environment and start to feel stressed as they anticipate returning home for a holiday or break. When there is illness or death even a normally functioning family experiences stress.

Another way to help your son manage stress, because stress is only manageable not curable, is to recommend and to demonstrate the art of prioritizing. How do you organize the duties and responsibilities in your life? On paper? With numbers? Do you eliminate low priority items in times of duress? Model prioritizing behavior but let your son order his priorities and choose what he can or will eliminate. You can do this by email or in person. The students who are often most difficult to counsel are those who draw up detailed lists of their many responsibilities: a 40 page term paper, managing the performance of a major concert band, ending of a romantic relationship and an insufficient bank loan for his current tuition bill. After he writes the list he may refuse to eliminate any item even when the projected list of accomplishments is unrealistic. Are you willing to do a less than perfect and complete job? Are you willing to accept a less than perfect final product from your son? It is probable that if you are a perfectionist one or more of your children will also suffer from perfectionism. As you learn to adjust your needs to reduce stress, you can pass the tricks on to your son. It's advantageous to share with your son the struggles you have had and how you have learned to adjust and adapt.

Depression

1. **Recognize the symptoms of depression**
2. **Support your student's sense of optimism and positive self-esteem**
3. **Give perspective to the hard times**
4. **Get your student to professional help on campus, off campus or at home**

On the opposite side of the spectrum from the overachieving, highly motivated student is the student who becomes sad and depressed. Not all students who are feeling down would be diagnosed as clinically depressed, a disease indicating more severe and enduring symptoms, but all students at one time or another may feel down or blue. I have found that students today have a great deal of difficulty coping with disappointment and problems.

What causes depression.

Many experiences unique to this age group result in temporary lows. Individual events like the end of a sexual relationship that may not be as significant the third or fourth time around take on great import the first time they occur. The end of a first love affair almost always causes a more dramatic blue period for a young man or woman. The good news about the majority of students who do seek counseling at the end of a first love is that their symptoms tend to be short lived, although intense. Most of us can remember the tears and sadness involved in the ending of our first love affair. The fact that we have lost our heart more than once doesn't help our daughter in the throes of her first break up. Remembering to understand her emotions from her innocent point of view rather than our more experienced perspective, we can however help her keep it in context and provide hope that she will love and be loved again. It is important to listen, to be sympathetic to her pain and yet maintain optimism and hope. Each loving relationship adds to her storage of knowledge about what she may and may not eventually want in a partner leading to a life long love.

Older and wiser, she should be able to find a new individual to whom she will be close and special. I often advise that all old love affairs end; otherwise we would still be with that individual. Most of us have experienced a broken heart along the way. Love is as much timing as anything. It can be the wrong person or the wrong time or the wrong place. We are all waiting for the right person at the right time and place. Supporting our daughter's sense of optimism and reinforcing her self-esteem, presently fragile, is critically important at this time.

What else might cause a student to feel depressed? Certainly the loss of a family member or friend through death can cause a period of mourning. Many students experience the death of someone close to them for the very first time during their college years. Particularly when a peer dies, an adolescent may question his own sense of immortality. Death is very uncomfortable to deal with for many in our culture and particularly difficult when as young adults we believe we will live forever. When reality destroys or changes expectations, depression can occur.

A college survey completed on our campus about ten years ago showed that second semester sophomore women were more emotionally down than any other group. We searched for an explanation. Often sophomore year is a time when students compare their expectations to their actual college experience. Reality is probably not measuring up to the idealistic expectations she might have fostered through her first year. Most of us go through periods of adjustment in a new environment. After the honeymoon period during which our eyes are blinded by the romance, we wake up to reality. We then readjust our expectations. Hopefully we can then accept the new job, education or partner. Depression can set in when reality doesn't match our unrealistic expectations, and we are unable to adjust and adapt. When your daughter's expectations aren't met she may make changes, adapt to the situation or become depressed. Your daughter's roommate has told a secret to her enemy. Her sorority sister pursues her boyfriend. Her chemistry professor tells her she will never make it into medical school. She doesn't get the lead in the spring musical. She loses the election for student council representative. One or more of these events requires your daughter to adjust.

Individual disappointments or a collection of negative experiences can cause one to sink into the doldrums. Bottom line is that life is filled with ups and downs. It is important to assist her in putting negative times into perspective and encourage her to never lose hope. We need to acknowledge the sadness of a particular period at the same time as we reassure her of the hopefulness of tomorrow.

Signs of significant depression

What should you do when your son is eating too much or too little, sleeping all the time or not at all, cutting classes, abusing drugs and alcohol, neglecting his personal hygiene by not showering or not keeping his clothes and room clean, or cutting himself off from friends? Sometimes a young person is irritable and angry. As a layperson we may not associate irritability with depression because the person has some animation rather than passive sadness. Don't be fooled into thinking there is no depression present.

It is difficult to respond to someone who is irritable, angry and answers every suggestion with a "been there, done that" and "it doesn't work." Such students have taught me that irritability is another mask of depression. Your son's anger is really self-directed but he projects the anger onto others, especially you, his helpful parents. That may be his only way to express his emotions at the time. Of course stress can also initiate the downward spiral into depression.

Prevention

Prevention or at least amelioration of symptoms includes regular exercise, rest and eating patterns. It is also important for a student who is moving into depression to stay in contact with loved ones and friends. Social isolation is a symptom of depression and also contributes to its continuation. The reality is that most of the time depression will naturally abate after a few months whether it is a period of feeling down or blue or a more serious clinical depression. Whatever the degree of sadness, parents need to assist their son in finding help in order to move through this period.

Your response

If any of these symptoms become severe, it is important to make sure that your son makes contact with counseling services either on or off campus. If he becomes unable to meet his daily responsibilities, bring him home for a few weeks, a semester or longer, and make sure he receives professional help. There is a varied world of therapy and medication and if he can still get to class and concentrate on his work, he may be able to continue school.

How to help your students get the help they need?

1. **Come see your student in person**
2. **Explain your concerns**
3. **Cite specific behavior**
4. **Lead your student to professional help**

When your daughter is showing signs of disordered eating or depression or other unusual behavior or affect, how do you get her to the help she needs? This is a very difficult task. She will often refuse not only your offers of help but also angrily deny that she has a problem at all. What is a parent to do? Frequently parents at this point will call the dean or the counseling center to express their concern. That first step may make you feel better but what then? Some parents expect the college professionals to call in their daughter to discuss her problem. This approach is rarely successful. Most students resent the intrusion of the college official, possibly a stranger, and will continue to deny the existence of any problem so that she is no closer to getting help.

For the everyday college concerns, the most important intervention you can make is coming in person to see your son. The visit will serve a dual purpose. You can assess first hand the severity of the problem, and you can facilitate his contact with a professional. Take him for lunch and conversation. Tell him of your concerns directly by citing specific behaviors such as a despairing email, low grades at midterm, phone calls to his room when his roommate repeatedly says he is sleeping, or large sums of money being withdrawn for unsubstantiated expenses. Explain whatever evidence has brought you to this level of concern to cause you to visit. You want to explain that you understand that this behavior can be indicative of problems and you are concerned about his well-being. You want to practice good listening skills and open the door for your son to share the emotions behind his behaviors. Often the few behaviors you have become aware of from a distance are only the tip of the iceberg of his problems, which is why you want to make the visit and make your own more complete observations to draw thorough conclusions. It gives you the opportunity to ask general questions and observe his physical condition, the condition of his living environment and his interactions with his friends. If your visit confirms your belief that your son is in need of professional help, you can facilitate that contact by suggesting he call the counseling center for an appointment, sitting with him while he calls the counseling center, or escorting him to the counseling center. Start with the least intrusive suggestion and work your way up the list depending on the severity of the problem and the immediacy of his need for help.

Don't ask someone else to either check on your son's current mental state or make the counseling connections for him. My counseling center staff was instructed not to take an appointment made for a student by a third party. The majority of students will not keep an appointment made for them by others. If your son is unwilling to make his own appointment, he is not going to be open to the counseling process. So I am suggesting leading your son to help.

It is really important to be fully apprised of your own family mental health history. Depression and anxiety and other disorders can run in families. If there is a history of these disorders in your family and you start to see symptoms in your son, it becomes even more critical to make that visit. If you live a great distance from campus, a trusted family friend or relative may offer their services, or in less dire circumstances wait for your son's visit home over a break.

The one exception is when your son has expressed suicidal intent. This is an emergency and you should

immediately contact a college official so an intervention can be made.

I often advise parents that referrals are important but not always successful. Frequently I hear from a variety of sources on the college campus over time that a particular individual's behavior suggests bulimia or depression or substance abuse. A faculty member may mention a student who has missed an excessive number of classes or appears glassy-eyed when he is in class. Another student may visit the counseling center to ask how to get their friend to stop vomiting her food after every meal. Or I might even observe a particular student's excessive drinking at a sporting event. What I suggest is to cite the behavior of concern and facilitate a visit to the counseling center.

Unless your son is in imminent danger to himself or someone else, don't be disappointed if he doesn't immediately follow up by making an appointment. A young woman's mother insisted on making an appointment with a counselor in her hometown. That very same week she made her own appointment with me because she wanted to choose her own therapist outside of her mother's purview. Her mother's behavior motivated her to make her own arrangements. She came to the counseling center to discuss a sexual assault that had occurred when she was fourteen. We continued our counseling relationship until her college graduation three and a half years later. This example not only demonstrates leading a student to help but also the not untypical time lag between a traumatic incident and professional assistance. Individuals often do not seek help immediately following a trauma.

The possibility of help for a college landmine may come about at some time in the future. Your student may not make the connection between her behavior, distress and available help. As her parent, you must let her know that you acknowledge the existence of a problem and plant the seed that you think professional help is warranted and will support her in receiving that help.

What is probably most frustrating to a parent is accepting the adult status of your son and that he makes his own decisions about his behavior and its consequences. If his mental capacity is not diminished by illness, he is in control of when, where and how he receives help, if at all.

You don't have this control over any other adult. You only have control over your own behavior. If your son chooses to continue his behavior and doesn't seek help in spite of your cajoling or ordering, the best thing is to seek help for yourself. A therapist can help you accept the limitations of your influence in your son's life.

This is a chapter that I know too much about. If you have a daughter, she will at one time confront problems involving eating, anxiety, and depression. And unfortunately it is likely that she will struggle with at least one of these troubles and the worst part for you, as a parent, is that she will deal with it alone.

Over-eating, under-eating, anxiety, depression, low self-esteem, all of these problems can easily intermingle until it is difficult to separate them. I am going to talk about eating disorders because I have seen too many friends who have been afflicted. Their bodies have given physical cries for help and they cannot be ignored. This book largely encourages you to allow your child to have space to work out most things for herself. I agree completely with this

166

idea, but there are some problems that get out of hand and need to be confronted by the family.

Here is my advice to the parent. Be alert. Be active. If you have an open relationship with your daughter, you have less to worry about. Be wary of her environment; if friends or roommates have problems with eating, her chances of following their patterns might increase. If your daughter shows any of the warning signs, like losing a significant amount of weight, obsessing over food, or going to the bathroom after every meal, get a book, talk to a professional, understand what you may be dealing with.

Remember, a serious eating disorder involves lying, even if your daughter is an honest person. The first step in recovery for a woman with an eating disorder is to admit to the problem. This is a very difficult thing to do because of the shame that is involved. My friends who told their families about their eating problems are the ones who have made the fullest recoveries because they were the most devoted to getting better. If you facilitate an open relationship with your daughter and are attentive in a

167

Linda L. Bips, Ed.D. with Jessica and Kristina Wallitsch

sensitive way, you may be able to help her before the warning signs develop into a serious disorder. Kristina

Chapter 10 Sex Drugs and Rock and Roll

1. **Learn about what is and isn't happening on college campuses today**
2. **Teach your student how to make good decisions by gathering information and assessing one's values**
3. **Know and share your own values about sexual activity and drug and alcohol use**
4. **Don't send mixed messages by saying one thing and doing the opposite**
5. **Share family risk factors with your student**
6. **Encourage exploration but discourage impulsive behavior changes**

For many of the parents reading this book today, you like me grew up in the 1960's. The media was filled with catch phrases like "free love," "legalize marijuana" and "long live the Beatles". The interesting question is how

169

those formative years have affected our parenting of our sons and daughters. Do we say to our students, "Do as I say not as I did?" Do we tell them what we did? Do we tell them, "Just say no?" Before we can answer these questions we need to look at then and now on campuses. For everything I say about college campuses today, the opposite is also true.

Sex

I experienced college in the 1960's and heard the calls for free love and feminist empowerment. Dorm rules changed from 10 o'clock curfews on school nights first semester, which included Friday due to Saturday classes, to no curfews and no restrictions on who slept where by the time I was a senior. We thought it meant that the double standard was coming to an end and a woman could have sex under the same conditions as a man: have sex with whom she wanted, when she wanted and how she wanted including satisfaction guaranteed. First of all, the double standard never did die. Arriving on a college campus in the mid 80's, I was introduced to the term "walk of shame."

The "walk of shame" is the phrase to describe the walk a woman, wearing the same clothes that she wore out the night before, makes back from a male residence the morning after a party. The interpretation of the dress, location and timing is that the young woman has spent the night hooking up with a partner she has picked up the night before. When I have run workshops on the college campus titled the "walk of shame," students use the word "slut" to describe such a woman and the word "stud" to describe the man still asleep back in his residence. The double standard has not died in spite of all the hard work of feminists over the years. You may be asking is it feminist for women to have sex with multiple partners? You will have to answer this question. You must answer many questions and establish your own values before you consider passing advice onto your daughter. Bottom line is that you need to know your values.

What have I found on the college campuses of today in terms of actual behavior? I have found everything. Casual sex is alive and well. Some students have sex with multiple partners with little to no emotional attachment. Some students have friendships that include sexual behavior and some students treat sex as a service, for example the young women who give their male friends oral sex as a casual favor. "Hook ups" are common. This term is confusing when used in conversation. "Hooking up" can mean pairing off with a member of the opposite sex from the party pool for an evening and can but doesn't necessarily include intercourse. The numbers have changed. My college class in the 1960's was 2/3 male and 1/3 female. Many men went off campus for dates because of the low supply of females. Now there are more women than men on most college campuses. And there is no such thing as dating. Students don't wait for an invitation for a date but travel in groups and come together in party scenes that look just like the 60's. Fueled by alcohol, students have impaired judgment and may then engage in unplanned or even unwanted sexual activity.

There are also students who view intercourse as an act of emotional intimacy and require a committed relationship before engaging in sex with another person. They want to experience sex with someone special. Even women who later have multiple partners reminisce about the first time with someone emotionally important. A student may value her status as a virgin and only engage in sexual contact that excludes intercourse. The argument of what is sex was made even more ambiguous by our past president's definitions. Some students are not opposed to premarital sex but haven't found the right first time. They feel that it becomes more and more difficult to become sexually active. I have met with some senior women who would like to experience a sexual relationship and feel burdened by their virginity. This circumstance is disturbing to them but they maintain a desire for a meaningful first time encounter and become more guarded about casual sex.

Regrettable sex/Date rape

Unfortunately, alcohol and sexual behavior can result in two disturbing outcomes. The first is called regrettable sex. I am not talking about the quality of the sexual encounter but the fact that it occurred at all. Students seduced by alcohol may get carried away with the surge of hormones and have sexual intercourse. Hours later she awakes and looks at her bed partner and thinks what did we do? If she remembers what happened, she may regret her participation. The partner is probably someone with whom she did not plan to have sex and without the influence of alcohol someone with whom she wouldn't have had sex. This can happen to men or women. Getting carried away with the dancing and the drinking and the convenience of the bedroom can lead to a sexual encounter when none was intended. There is a college myth that these circumstances lead to an accusation of rape. In my experience this is rarely the case in campus rape charges. Women who have experienced regrettable sex are not the women who claim date rape. What is the difference between regrettable sex and date rape?

Date rape is a sad fact on the college scene. Date rape is forced sexual intercourse by someone a woman knows. The act may or may not include violence. A woman who is incapable of saying no to forced intercourse is still a victim. She may not be able to say no because of fear, alcohol or having been drugged with roofies, a drug that induces a state of amnesia, or something similar. I don't believe that date rape only started happening in the 90's on college campuses. Rape has always existed in our society. I do believe, however, that more people are willing to talk about rape since the media and college campuses address the topic directly. There is still a reluctance to press charges, and statistics are always inadequate because rape is underreported.

Some women will talk to a college counselor about the emotional toll of the experience but not confide in anyone else because of the stringent federal laws that require all other administrators and faculty to report the crime. Most college campuses have worked hard at counteracting the negative impressions of the administrative handling of rape as detailed in fiction and fact which conclude that college administrators wish to cover up the existence of date rapes on their campuses. This has not been my experience. One reality is that other students may subject a woman who reports a rape to verbal harassment. Fear of such reprisal keeps many women from reporting or prosecuting the perpetrator.

Unfortunately unwanted sexual activity is not limited to college campuses or young adults. A support group for victims of unwanted sexual activity that I conducted had a majority of members who had experienced rape or molestation long before arriving on a college campus. These incidents occurred when they were children in their own neighborhood or when they were young adolescents at such places as summer camps. Although the number of women who were pre-college victims of abuse is small, most of these women have never confided in their parents. Our beliefs and knowledge about our children's experiences including wanted or unwanted sexual activity or their use of alcohol/drugs or other illegal activities are not always accurate. Some children are involved in activities at a young age, willingly or unwillingly, before they have the cognitive ability to make good choices or sometimes the verbal ability to confide and seek the guidance of their parents. As parents we can never assume that we know everything about our student's entire social history.

Behavior and values

"Anything goes" on the college campus of today. Your advice to your son on this topic has a great deal to do with the values you have instilled in him over the last eighteen years. Many parents of today are more open to discussing sexual values with their sons and daughters, but we still often struggle with saying the right thing to provide our son with guidelines to healthy and fulfilling sexual behavior. There are two possible reasons that we may experience this struggle. We may not know what we want to say, the right answer. Also we may want to maintain our son's attention to what we are saying and not lose him after our first sentence. We want him to be receptive to our message and not tune us out.

Many times our values are reflected more in our judgmental statements about others than in explanations of our own behavior. Countless times students have told me that they have no knowledge of their parents' sexual behavior during young adulthood. This does not seem to be information that most parents readily share with their young adults. We might use the occasional television program like

"The Cosby Show" or "Roseanne" to begin a discussion, but many of us are still embarrassed and inhibited when it comes to talking about sex. We often sound like our parents who refrained from discussing sex at all. Sometimes parents have had particular experiences in their youth that translate into clear messages for their student about sexual behavior. A woman, who gave birth to a child during her college years and gave the baby up for adoption, may adopt a strong abstinence message for her daughter as she enters college. The mother hopes to protect her daughter from the painful consequences of her previous behavior.

Making good decisions

What can we tell our students about sex? First of all I have written this chapter so you can have a more accurate picture of what is happening on the college campus of today. Some of you may be saddened, disgusted, skeptical or have had your perceptions confirmed. Again I remind you that for everything I say the opposites are also true, and this is not meant to be a comprehensive guide to sex on campus. The most important message to give your sons and daughters about their sexual behavior is the importance of making good decisions. Decision-making is a skill and is the most important skill for all the hot topics of campus life. Decision-making includes taking an inventory of one's values, seeking information about the topic and combining the two into behavior that allows one to stay true to the person she is and be comfortable with the resulting behavior and its consequences.

Exploring values

Your conversation should include your values about sexual behavior. It is astounding to me how many students believe that their parents never had premarital sex or had sex with more than one partner. Every generation seems to believe that they have invented sex and all the desires that initiate sexual contact. Tell your students what choices you made and why. Did you have premarital sex? What were your criteria for making decisions to be sexual? Where did these values come from – religious beliefs, physical considerations, philosophical thoughts about humanity, social restrictions, family values or negative or positive experiences? If your values have changed since adolescence, why have they changed? It is important to share as much information and your thought processes as you comfortably can.

This kind of values education has probably been going on in your home for a very long time. There is probably not much that you will say just before your son leaves for college that is going to change the foundation that you have laid for the last eighteen years. I have worked with many students who have been confused by their parents' behavior. One young woman told me about her father's lifelong view that premarital sex is wrong yet he put several boxes of condoms in her college packing boxes. Make your messages clear. It is, however, important to make sure that your daughters and sons have good reliable information about not only birth control but also disease prevention.

Information

Information is the second part of good decision making. In the 1960's, birth control changed dramatically with the advent of the pill, amusingly portrayed in the movie "Prudence and the Pill." Women students were predominantly responsible for obtaining the pregnancy protection, which was not always easy. In our sleepy college town, the local gynecologist still required the fiction, if not fact, of a forthcoming wedding for him to write the required prescription for birth control. Condoms were not frequently used during that time, and many couples relied on such unreliable techniques as withdrawal and the rhythm method, when couples only had sex during the "safe" times of the women's menstrual cycle. A professor in human sexuality recently told a joke to her class about coitus interruptus that lost its humor since students had no idea what the term meant. Such practices resulted in high numbers of unwanted pregnancies that were sometimes terminated by doctors providing illegal abortions at motels or were the impetus for "shotgun weddings." Today there is a large, readily available supply of information about the use of condoms, in addition to other forms of birth control, to protect against sexually transmitted diseases. In the 80's, I found myself in the college president's office discussing the sale and distribution of condoms, a situation I could never have imagined from my former life experiences. Certainly the arrival of acquired immune deficiency syndrome (AIDS) on college campuses eliminated the reservations about frank talk about sex. AIDS brought safer sex to the forefront of consciousness, and it is not uncommon today in a date rape situation for a woman to insist that the perpetrator use a condom if she can't prevent the act. Students also typically have access to the morning after pill so that if she has had unprotected sex for any reason including lack of planning she can terminate any possible pregnancy. The legalization of abortion has permitted any woman to terminate unwanted pregnancies in a safe medical procedure. Students need to seek methods of protection from pregnancy and disease if they plan to be sexually active. It is always important that a student be able to make an informed decision about sexual activity rather than being coerced by peer pressure, personal pressure or violence.

How to give advice

So how do you advise your daughter? What do you say to your son? You cannot be sure of her choice or be responsible for his sexual choices. They may not have made these decisions and are still exploring or they just aren't telling you their choices. More about the how to's at the end of this chapter.

> This is what not to say, it doesn't work: "Don't have sex. You'll have plenty of time to have sex later. You have better things to do now. Boys and sex may seem fun, but you are not going to school to have that much fun!"
>
> Kerin junior

Drugs

Illegal drugs became prevalent on the college campuses of the 1960's. Drugs of the sixties included marijuana, hashish, LSD. There was also awareness, if not always a ready supply, of drugs like heroin and cocaine. Frequently students used amphetamine/speed perhaps acquired as a diet control, to stay awake to pull an all-nighter to study for that exam or finish that paper. All these substances were illegal then as they are now. Of course alcohol, the legal drug as of age 21, has always been part of the college campus culture except in the rare exception, a dry campus. The questions of use, abuse and addiction persist.

What's available today? All and more. The same drugs appear: alcohol, marijuana, cocaine, heroin, and speed. Plus there are more drugs available to this generation. Ecstasy is synthetically produced and is frequently found at dance parties called raves. Shrooms are a form of mushroom that when smoked create a high. Ritalin and Adderal are legally prescribed drugs for students with attention deficit disorder (ADD/ADHD). The purpose of these drugs is to assist a student with disabilities to maintain focus for studying. Students without ADD buy the drug and use it to create a buzz or, like the speed of the 60's, to stay awake and focus on schoolwork into the late hours. But let's not be naïve. Many students come to college having already sampled alcohol and many other drugs. Sadly the opportunities for experimenting have moved down into our high school and middle school populations. Your son may know the facts earlier in his life than you did but he hasn't developed the emotional skills and maturity to override his friends' invitations to try ecstasy, Ritalin and Adderal. Many students come to college with their drug and alcohol habits already firmly established during their high school years. Some have already spent time in a rehabilitation center as an outpatient or even an inpatient.

Recent annual surveys by the Cooperative Institutional Research Program, UCLA Higher Education indicate that around 50% of first year college students are drinking beer in the year before entering college and around 10% are smoking cigarettes. About 1 in 3 of recent college freshman support the legalization of marijuana. Year to year the numbers vary but there is always a problem. Alcohol abuse has been a major concern for our colleges and universities. Based on the statistics of a nationally distributed report, eight universities were granted major long-term grants to solve the problems of alcohol on campuses, particularly binge drinking, 5 drinks in a row for a man and 4 drinks in a row for a woman. It is not enough to "get a buzz on," but to drink to drunkenness in the shortest amount of time possible by pounding down drinks.

Alcohol abuse has changed from the 60's when one's roommate would be vomiting into the wastebasket all night to today's tragic reports of alcohol poisoning sometimes resulting in death. Does your son know the facts – about alcohol poisoning and how it happens and the potency of certain kinds of liquor. On a recent college stop in Japan, a young woman partook in a free sake hour where she drank as many sake shots as she could, resulting in alcohol poisoning. She stated she had no idea that the alcohol content of sake was any different than beer or wine. If you don't know the information, get it from the multitude of literature that is out there. Some good sources appear at the end of this book. Just saying no to drugs will not work. Prohibition has never worked so be knowledgeable and offer facts, not sermons, to your son. Clearly it is important if there is a history of alcohol/drug addiction in your family to make your son aware of his increased risk. Alcoholism is a family disease.

One of the most controversial drugs for young adults and their parents is marijuana. In the late 1960's, pot appeared on most college campuses as a substitute for alcohol. Many students believe that they are wiser and more sensitive to the intensity of life when they smoke weed. Other students smoke to mask the pain of depression. The problem becomes the chronic smoker who smokes regularly throughout her day - before class, after class, evenings, mornings, anytime and all the time. Many of these students have parents who started smoking in the 60's and have continued that practice. Some families even smoke together. Again this is a values question. If your family lifestyle includes regular pot smoking you can probably count on your daughter to continue that practice. You and your daughter should become informed about the consequences of marijuana on one's physical and mental well being now and long term. In my early years as director of the college counseling center, a student came to request a medical leave. He appeared extremely depressed and had stopped going to classes. A few weeks after the medical leave was processed and he had moved off campus, another student unintentionally disclosed to me that the source of this student's depression was his continuous pot smoking. Which came first - the depression or the marijuana? I may not know but I do know that the combination ended his college career.

What to do?

Ask your son to refrain from changing his behavior for the first semester of college. I like to call it stop, look, and listen (the old street crossing mantra). Stop doing any new behaviors. Look around and see what others are doing or not doing. Listen to why others are doing or not doing certain behaviors. After a semester of observing and questioning others, either verbally or through research, he will be better prepared to make informed decisions about his behavior without becoming a victim of impetuosity. Those first few golden weeks of college behavior may be determined by the need to belong, a strong human motivator especially in new environments and for this age group, rather than one's own convictions. The first six weeks of college have been called the red zone – on alert. Many students are vulnerable because they want to fit in to the college scene. They make the mistake of joining in with the sex or drugs or new politics or religions before they have clarified their values or thought through the consequences of such behavior. This is a wonderful time for exploration both in informal and formal settings. Many of my current spiritual beliefs originated in an introductory course on religion taken my first year in college. Intellectually your son can examine his beliefs and the beliefs of others but advise him to postpone commitment to the new until he has passed through the transition time. Encourage your son to take advantage of every opportunity to examine and discuss his values at the same time as you discourage him from trying on these new behaviors. Every year in the counseling center, I see the victims of impulsive new behavior - the young woman who felt she needed to have sexual intercourse with that handsome senior in order to gain the desperately sought popularity or the young man who wanted to run with the in crowd by starting a daily marijuana habit. These men and women regret their impulsive first choices, and sometimes the damage is insurmountable and they leave school by their own choice or due to disciplinary or academic consequences. Small schools are notoriously difficult places to alter reputations after those first impressions. You may want to help your daughter understand the preference to avoid rather than act and regret.

Remember the system of good communication. You should listen to affect and content. Tell your student your feelings. Specify the behavior of concern and suggest alternative behaviors. If your student is in immediate danger, personally take him for professional help. If he refuses to listen, seek help for you.

The Beatles are still the kings of rock and roll

One of the more pleasurable aspects of raising children today is the opportunity to revisit the music of the past. While driving car pool when Kristina was nine, "In the Still of the Night" came on the radio. I started singing along and she asked, "Mommy, how do you know the words to that song?" I replied, "This is my music." I have been delighted to be reintroduced to Joni Mitchell and expand my repertoire to Cat Stevens as she shared the music of her teen years. Remakes or originals, it is nice to share appreciation of music, something our parents refused to do with the introduction of rock and roll that they said wouldn't last. I hope you too are enjoying these moments together.

It is important for parents to be open with their children. If you communicate with your child often, there is no reason this should change when your child goes to college. It is important to be open when your child tells you something. If you are critical of your child or their friends, your child will probably not continue to communicate with you. Even if your first reaction is "You did WHAT?" do not let your child know that you feel that way. Just listen, and take a moment before responding. Jessica

This chapter is an interesting one to write about because I assume my crowd in college lived in the fast lane. I think that a little experimentation is healthy for the typical student. I started trying things out in high school like the average teenager. My parents were active in my life and therefore probably knew what I was up to most of the time. I think the exposure was a good thing because I already knew

where to draw the line by the time I got to college. Kristina

Chapter 11 Saying Good-bye

1. **Discuss the upcoming separation**

2. **Model the ability to have contradictory emotions**

3. **Ask your student to talk about the transition**

4. **Only give advice when it is requested**

5. **Tell your student how you feel about him and his leaving**

6. **Be yourself**

7. **Talk about your excitement for his future**

8. **Talk about how home will be the same and different**

9. **Give your student future meeting times to anticipate**

10. **Attend to the feelings of your other children**

Preparation

One of the most difficult parts of going away to college for your son or daughter is the anticipation of leaving home and separating from you. When I ask student audiences some of their reasons for going to college, "getting away from our parents" is a popular response. Although they are cheering with their peers, they may be teary or irritable with you because of their mixed feelings. As Jessica and I went through the arduous college search, I frequently would discuss the upcoming separation. A full year before it became an actuality, we started talking about her going away to college and what that would mean to both of us. It got to the point where she would jokingly say, "Mom, don't say the "c" word". It often made us both very sad.

Contradictory emotions

I have explained to my daughters that although I feel sad at their leaving, I also am excited about the opportunities awaiting them. As they have grown and wandered, I have repeatedly expressed my sadness and joy. First was the departure of my oldest daughter for her first year of college at a school two hours from home. The next year my younger daughter left for boarding school one and one half-hours from my now empty nest. The next spring my older daughter participated in a college semester on a ship going around the world limiting our communications to her phone calls when in port, my occasional fax to the middle of the Indian ocean and letters that often took weeks to arrive with old news. After applying to college in California, my youngest daughter moved only one hour away to a major city university. She traveled her first summer and continued to live in the city through the summer following her sophomore year, never coming home again for more than a few weeks. Following college, my oldest daughter went to Africa for a year of teaching. And the leave takings continued to England, California and another trip around the world. Who knows where they will go next? I can be sad, shed tears, and yet encourage and want them to leave.

For all of us having contradictory feelings is very difficult, but for late adolescents ambiguity is intolerable and confusing. In my early years of college counseling, I told a student that she could both love and be angry with her father at the same time. She was amazed. Young adults are often only capable of dichotomous thinking. Things are either good or bad and your response to their leaving for college with sadness may require an explanation that you also feel excitement and encouragement. Your modeling by expressing what seems like contradictory emotions gives permission to your student to experience and express his own varied feelings about leaving home. This will help with the transition as well as help him develop the next level of intellectual capacity – abstract thinking.

It is very important to communicate several things to your student as you anticipate his departure for college, and later when he leaves for a semester abroad or moves on into life following his college graduation. It is very important to ask your son to talk about the transition. The communication of fears does much to allay them. Countless times students leave my office "feeling better" and I have only listened. I listened intently and openly without judgment but I only listened. Too often as parents we feel the need to do more than listen - fix, advise or criticize when just listening will do. Remember you are a consultant but listening comes first. Only give advice when it is requested.

What to tell your student

It is important to tell your student that you love her. Many of you probably at this point are saying "Yeah, yeah, yeah. They already know that. Why do we need to say it?" The sad truth is that too few parents tell their children in words that they love them. My daughter's high school friend needed her mother to say, "I love you." It is very important for your students to hear you say it, not just to know it. If you haven't verbalized your love to her before, you might think about starting today. Too many students visiting the counseling center aren't sure both parents truly love them. It's important for your student to know that you love her.

It's important to tell your child that you will miss them. It's all right to be sad. It's all right to shed tears. It's all right to experience the bittersweet aspects of the moment. When I took my younger daughter to boarding school, others advised me not to let her see me cry. I was disturbed by this advice and gave it considerable thought. When I brought her to soccer camp a week before school began, tears came to my eyes as I hugged her and said good-bye.

She cried too and we talked about what our tears were about. This was a child who because she did not want to leave me, a single parent, alone, contemplated not going to boarding school which in every other way she wanted to attend. As I told her then and have told her many times since then that the fact that she considers my needs means a great deal to me. On the other hand, I would be very disappointed if she chose not to take advantage of some wonderful opportunities because she felt she needed to take care of her mom who is perfectly capable of taking care of herself even though I miss her. Her response to my tears was, "Mom, I would have thought you were sick if you didn't cry when you said good-bye". So I guess most importantly be yourself and tell your student what you will miss and talk about what may be painful for both of you. Your boundary is to stop your needs or feelings from dominating your student's choices.

Talk also about your excitement for these upcoming college years. Don't say, "These are the best years of your life". Our college memories may be rose colored by hindsight. She may not feel like these are the best days of her life when she is staying up all night to finish a paper, just broke up with her first lover or is facing disciplinary action by the dean for underage drinking. It is wonderful, however, to anticipate the excitement of new things that will happen at college - the new people she will meet, the new academic disciplines she will learn and the hopes that she will find an intellectual mentor for her future.

Finally, talk about what in the future will be different at home and what will be the same. Do not give her room over to her little sister the minute she's out the door, and resist the urge to turn her room into your office. You'll be surprised at how often she may be home that first year. Most schools have fall and Thanksgiving breaks. The mid year break is usually about a month. She needs to feel like she still has a place in your home both in terms of physical and emotional space. Talk about the next time you will see your daughter. Remember students should not come home for weekends prior to that first fall break. Time at home interferes with the college transition and a good adjustment. As you leave your child at college that first day, give your daughter future milestones as something to look forward to when times get rough those first few weeks of school. Upon her first visit home at fall break or Thanksgiving, make it special with favorite foods, family time and a transition back into the home environment.

> "Telling my family goodbye feels about like it would feel to have my eye sockets scraped clean each time I do it, but every time I go home I am ready to leave again, get back to my own life, and say goodbye. Sadomasochism, or the great freedom of being 20 years old? There are clear downfalls to both. I will always miss home.
>
> Kerin junior

Siblings have feelings, too

As we waved goodbye to Jess in front of her residence hall, Kristina started to sob. I remember the road sign said fifteen miles to the nearest city and she was still crying as we reached the city highway. We shared our feelings but I felt I needed to comfort Kris and drive. Back home I sat in Jessica's semi-empty room and allowed my tears to flow. Don't be deceived by the sibling who expresses joy instead. Remember the difficulty of ambivalent feelings and look for other moments of sadness or anger. Use these moments as an opportunity to help your younger child understand that he too can feel contradictory emotions about the same event.

Family illness

One year a young man dropped by my office the day before a scheduled exam to let me know that he had to leave early for a scheduled trip to see his grandmother for the weekend because of a medical emergency. His grandmother recovered. A week later another elderly family member had an emergency, and John was again expected to come home, this time for an extended period to assist with the family needs for caretakers and drivers. John missed several weeks of classes at a critical time in the semester. College calendars and deadlines are not always as flexible as one may like and serious thought must be put into both academic and family demands.

One of the most difficult counseling situations occurs when a parent discovers that he/she is terminally ill and subsequently dies. Some parents keep this information from their student. Other parents share the information with the insistence that the student not leave college to be home with them, while others ask their student to be home during their last months. One student came to college knowing that her mother's death was imminent. Her mother lapsed into a coma a few days before the daughter was to leave. Just hours after she said her good-byes, her mother quietly passed on.

These are very difficult times for these young people. I do not recommend a standard approach to these situations. So much depends on the parent, the student, the relationship, the illness, and the timing. Most importantly, the parent and student need to talk about the situation, their individual needs and desires and come to a solution that is the best for everyone involved. There is no one size fits all. Recently an upper-class student chose to take a semester off from college to accompany her grandmother through her treatment for cancer. Communication will help you arrive at the best solution if you should ever have to deal with a similar difficult situation.

Move in day

This will certainly be an exciting day for your family. It will be a milestone in the life of your son as he moves away from your home, maybe for the first time. It will be an emotional day with the possibility of short tempers, tears or silence. Pitch in with the moving in process. Let your son go through the lines to pick up his keys and orientation materials. Help carry his boxes up to the assigned room but unpack only at his direction. Allow your student time alone to get to know his roommate(s). Offer to run errands to the nearby convenience store for snacks or a department store for one more lamp. Maybe have a nice lunch with your family and walk around and enjoy the campus. Say good-bye. Find a private spot for a brief farewell. Tell your son you will look forward to his call some time over the next few days, and leave.

If your travels are long and you must spend the night, do not plan on spending additional time on campus. Your son will be very busy with activities, setting up his room, meeting his advising group, hallmates, and faculty. This is his time and it is very important for him to begin the process of becoming part of the college community. Remember that good advice we received when our child started nursery school? Today it's the same good advice that we all received fifteen years ago.

Close the door, get in the car and go home.

When I said, "Mom, don't say the "c" word," I was very anxious, nervous and excited about the prospect of going away to college. By not saying the "c" word, I felt that I could forget about the anxiety I was feeling until the day I was actually leaving. Although this strategy may work for some people, it was not positive for me and I would not recommend it. As in any other life situation, communication is very important. I should have dealt with my anxiety by discussing it and learning how to deal with it.

I also remember how important it was to me that it was not going to be forever until I was going to see my family again. I knew I could call them when I needed to talk, and they would come and visit me at school if I was missing them. I tried to come home as seldom as possible, especially the first two years. It helped me to realize that it was important to stay at school but that my family would come to visit if I needed them.

I still remember my first day at college and saying goodbye to my family. I was sad to see them leave and cried for a few minutes afterwards. Then I left my new room and walked around meeting new people and getting acquainted with my new environment. It was good to stay busy and to immediately get interested and excited about my new college life. As a freshman, keeping busy is an easy concept considering all of the orientation meetings and activities usually prepared for freshman at most colleges. My suggestion is to encourage your child to communicate their feelings, get involved and stay busy, stay at college and see going away to the "c word" as an exciting adventure. Jessica

I remember crying as my parents pulled away from my dorm. But I also remember going back to my dorm, showering, and heading out with friends to go to a party. The easiest goodbye is a gradual one. The best advice I can give to students going into their freshman year is to find a pre-frosh program. Most schools provide these opportunities before orientation begins. I went on a three-day camping trip and ended up meeting friends that I kept all four years of school. I was at school before the rush of students came in and I told my mom I'd see her in a few days. By the time I had to say the real goodbye, I was already beginning to feel at home. Kristina

Chapter 12 Myths – Four Years and the Ideal College

1. **Consider time out for students**
2. **Spread courses over more than four years**
3. **Have your student consider deferring the start of college for a year**
4. **Transferring is not the end of the world**
5. **Keep all options open when considering transferring**

Current national statistics indicate that less than 50 % of students finish a bachelor's degree in the traditional four years. Your student may need to take a time out, to space his courses out over more than eight semesters, to defer college admission or transfer. Today there are many reasons that students take five or more years to complete their college education. We want our student to graduate, but the four-year ideal isn't the only way. As parents we are often afraid that if our son leaves college without completing his bachelor's degree, he may never go back. Sadly, that may be true, but the reality is that some students do need time and many do eventually finish their degree. Let's examine some of these reasons.

Time out

I remember a young man who spent his first year maximizing his social experience and minimizing his academic endeavors. At the end of the first year of college he had a grade point average that didn't force his withdrawal but would make his continued progress an uphill battle. He decided not to return to the college in the fall. He lived at home and attended a few classes at a local community college. Over the years, he stayed in touch with me through email. In hindsight he felt he wasn't emotionally ready for the full college experience. He had become involved in a social crowd that frequently smoked marijuana. His immaturity and some depression made him vulnerable to peer pressure, and his academics became unimportant. Under the restrictions of his home environment and a part time job, his behavior changed and he began to again perform well in school. At the end of his sophomore year, he moved on to a residential state university where he successfully completed a bachelor's degree four years after he originally started college. The initial college experience was too much freedom combined with his immaturity.

Sometimes students are just not ready for the rigors of college academics and don't take the coursework seriously. A low grade point average the first semester or first year can be difficult to raise in subsequent years. Some students benefit from a minimum wage job and the rules of home living. They learn about the privilege of attending college at a campus with the full smorgasbord of education and social activities and about the impact a college degree will have on their future careers and lifestyles. Sometimes students, returning after a timeout, may decide to change their social milieu upon returning to school. Their first year cohorts may have abused alcohol or drugs or prioritized social life over academics. With time out, the student can reorganize his priorities.

Sometimes students need a time out for other reasons. Your daughter has been diagnosed with an eating disorder or your son is battling depression. College may be the wrong place at the wrong time. My younger daughter needed a time out during the spring semester of her senior year – stress had taken a toll. She volunteered, worked part-time and focused her energy on her well-being. The next fall she took advantage of an opportunity to accompany me on a semester at sea program. Have you ever had someone zoom by you on the road only to meet up with them at the next red light? Graduating one year later makes little difference on the highway of life.

Spacing out academic requirements

There can be an advantage to spreading the academic requirements over a longer period of time. In our college, students are expected to take only four courses for the first two semesters. In order to complete the 34 courses required for graduation, every student on a regular fall, spring semester schedule over four years must take two semesters of five courses. Advisors never suggest five courses for a first year student because of all the additional adjustment factors we have been talking about. Frequently, however, a student with four courses finds himself in the second month of the semester in trouble in one or more of his courses. He may be falling behind in his work because of illness or poor management skills. The course content may be beyond his abilities. He may have a personality conflict with the instructor resulting in low performance. Continuing to put effort into a very difficult course will limit his resources for the other three courses. If he gets an F not only will he not get credit for the course but also he will severely damage his grade point average for the semester, which will have an impact on his entire college career including graduate school admissions and job applications. This student can still graduate in the prescribed four years by taking a course in summer school - possibly even in his hometown - at a less expensive institution. Summer school can also provide your son with the opportunity to concentrate on one course, such as foreign languages or math, that he might find to be more difficult when it is part of a four-course semester schedule. Another solution for a particular student may be reducing her course load every semester and always taking a summer course or adding on an additional semester or a year. My daughter transferred after her first year. She then had a major, a minor and a certification program to complete, and studied abroad for a semester. She finished college with more than the required number of courses in order to meet the requirements of all her programs. She took courses every summer and stayed on an extra semester to complete her student teaching. It is important for your student to successfully complete the degree. What could be more expensive than an unfinished education? The traditional four year, eight-semester model may not work for every student.

And why you have to be done with college in 4 years I will never know. I had a lot of friends graduate in May and now they are telling me, "I am working and have to get up early every morning and yadda yadda yadda." Why were they rushing? Why do we have to take 18 credits every semester? You can't give your full attention to all your classes. Why not just take 12 and who cares if you are there for an extra semester. You could get so much more and afford yourself a more comfortable pace and have more time to hang out and not have to constantly be so absorbed in only academics.

Gwen senior

Life is long. Students today are making their own college schedules and I meet many a student who proudly identifies himself as a five-year senior.

Deferred admission

What about the student who is graduating from high school but doesn't want to immediately attend college? The service academies routinely require high school graduates to take a postgraduate year at preparatory school before entering their first college year. First step is to check with the college of her choice about deferring admission for a year or maybe just a semester. One young woman chose to spend her first year out of high school in another country.

> After I graduated high school, I decided to spend a year in Israel volunteering and studying before I came to college. That 'year off' really proved to be a year on in terms of my personal growth and development. In immersing myself in another culture, it seemed like the next logical step after high school; rather, it was an opportunity and privilege that I could use to enhance my life. Although I was a top student in high school, I'm not sure that I would have been as prepared for college had

I not taken time off to explore myself. My year in Israel allowed me to enter college as a more focused and serious student, and as a result I believe I have had a more productive and altogether meaningful college experience.

Ilana senior

Your son may take a year to travel, do volunteer work or paid employment after high school and delay the start of college. During this time, it is important for him to contribute to his living expenses. I have taught some of these students who delayed entering college and am always impressed by their maturity and seriousness of purpose when they arrive at college after such an experience. Another student who transferred after one semester says,

I love how the Europeans do it. You have a couple years out of high school to just get to know yourself. I wasn't ready to be away at college but I felt like I had to go. How could I be the senior class president and not go straight off to college? I am sure if I had said that to my parents they would have been totally supportive, but I just couldn't say it. I couldn't tell other people that. I couldn't say I am going to take a year off before I go to college.

Gwen senior

All these alternatives are dependent on your student and your family's financial and lifestyle requirements.

Transferring

It can happen. Your son may have picked the wrong school. It could have been the right school at the time he made his decision, but it is the wrong school six months later. Or the college he saw in the admissions' viewbook or even on his tour doesn't resemble reality. Also students sometimes make their choices for the strangest reasons. One student told me she chose her college because everyone wore different kinds of footwear – sandals, sneakers, clogs and loafers. She interpreted shoe variety as an indication of diversity and independent thinking. Another student said he knew when he saw the flag in the front circle that this would be the school for him. A third student didn't even plan to visit one college, but her family stopped in need of a rest room on their way to another school in the area. After her immediate needs were met, she decided to take a tour and felt an instant connection. In this era of the super sell of college admissions, students become overwhelmed trying to compare gala apples to delicious apples rather than apples to oranges. They may apply to many schools. Jessica applied to six schools and, only three years later, Kristina applied to twelve. Your student's final choices may be from a list of very similar colleges. At her first semester break, Kris said the school she was attending was not the school that she thought it was. That isn't necessarily a bad thing. Many choices we make in life are from the outside and the reality once we are in our new school, job or house may not be to our liking. I love Boston cream donuts but am sorely disappointed when the filling is white cream instead of the vanilla custard I am expecting.

Also there is the February transfer phenomenon. Every year the rumors of large numbers of first year students transferring fly through the dorm. Some students send off for applications, visit friends at more favorable locations and decline the opportunity to register for fall classes or pick a roommate and room for the following year. I always recommend that a student keep all options open. He should explore the possibilities of other colleges, including filling out applications and obtaining faculty references. While he is applying to other schools, he should still put down his deposit, pick a room and a roommate and schedule classes for the next semester at her current college. As part of the decision making process, he should list not only the things at the new school that will improve upon his environment, but also those things which he likes about his current college. Students often get so concerned about finding a new place that corrects the flaws that they forget to look for a place that also continues to offer the characteristics they like. The student who hates the fact that her college town rolls up the sidewalks at sundown, may not find a park for running on that urban campus. Having the desired education program that provides early classroom experience may not be part of the new school's curriculum with an art therapy major. Sometimes students take for granted the characteristics they like and forget to look for them at the new college. It is important to visit the possible transfer colleges both for classes and a social night to find the best fit. The process should duplicate the most successful high school search. Your student may be a savvier shopper; however, he will still be an outsider until he actually registers and attends the new school.

In the sixties, most of us went to college and stayed. Our college attendance paralleled our father's loyalty to his company – retiring with a gold watch after fifty years. We graduated with a bachelor of arts degree after four years. If we did leave a college, we returned home and maybe attended a local community college or commuter school. Many students transfer today and it is not the end of the world. We sometimes place so much pressure on making the right college choice on May 1 of the senior year in high school that it is difficult for us to accept our student's later desire to give up the commitment we have all made to a particular institution. Early decisions are often made by sixteen or seventeen year olds who are experiencing rapid growth and change. Arriving one year later at the first choice campus at age eighteen may be a very disappointing experience. Transferring may be the best choice for your son or daughter.

My oldest daughter transferred after her first year. She transferred to a similar college for a variety of reasons, and it was a good move for her. She gained the opportunity to pursue a major in communications and participate in a strong dance program, neither of which existed at her first college. She had not articulated these needs when she made her initial college choice.

If your son transfers, maybe even mid year for his first year spring semester, it is important to revisit all the initial steps you made when you sent him off the first time. He has already spent several months away from home in a new environment that will make the newest separation easier. The disadvantage is that the other students currently in attendance at his new college have already had an extended period of time to get to know each other and to settle in. Your son is the only new kid. One of my students recently came to tell me that she thought her first winter break was plenty long enough and was anxious to get "home" (read college dorm) to see her friends after an extended absence. There is an already established social and residential scene and the transfer may have difficulty fitting in.

A student transferring into a new institution for their sophomore year has a different set of challenges and opportunities. The returning students have been away for the summer, and some of the friendships have shifted or may be unsteady with the passage of four months. Students are in new living situations. The upper-class students do try to live together in groups near their friends. The residence hall may offer a mix of students who are also new to each other and new to your son. The most important transition advice is to get involved. All clubs and organizations are making room for the new kids on campus so it is a good time for your son to join the newspaper, chorus or lacrosse intramural team. The very best way to meet new people is to work together on a task.

On my recent voyage with Semester at Sea, I started chatting with one of the many students on a field trip to Nara, Japan. As we explored our connections it became clear to us that Gwen had been one of my first year advisees four years before. What made this encounter unusual was that Gwen had left our college after her first semester freshman year to transfer to a large state university. When I met up with her, she explained that transferring had not been the solution to her first semester discontent, and we agreed to discuss her transfer – reasons and consequences.

I went home at Thanksgiving and was not very happy with college. A friend called me up and says what do you think about one of the state universities. We had looked there. She was at another college and she was not very happy either. So she said why don't we just apply. And I put no thought into it. I just said ok. I just applied over the Internet. I wasn't thinking. My boyfriend was there and so were a bunch of people from my high school. So I applied and I got in and she didn't. I didn't even know why I had applied.

I found out at Christmas time that I was accepted, and I moved out and didn't even tell my roommates anything. Now I totally regret the way I left. I couldn't deal with it at the time. I didn't want to be talked out of it. I didn't stop; I didn't slow down until the end of my spring semester. Then I thought, "What just happened?" I had the entire summer to think about it. At the holiday all my high school friends said, "I love college, I just love it." I didn't love it. I didn't know if there was something wrong with me or they were over dramatizing it. All I knew was that I didn't love it. Not that I was unhappy there, but I didn't love it. I always had the idea in my head that there was a perfect school and I was going to find it. And now I know that there is no such thing as a perfect school. You make the school fit your needs. You have your priorities and you make sure those priorities are met but beyond that it is up to you. I wasn't forming connections and that was my fault but at the time I held it against the school.

It is funny since I put so much planning into making my original decision about college. Oh now I want to go to the state university. Ok I will apply. I really found out at the end of the year that I wasn't that happy at this university either. OK what is going on here? Two schools. Something must be wrong with me. I started to think what do I want?

In hindsight, I think I should have just said, "Slow down". I was so caught up in the pace and making a decision and I couldn't say I just didn't know. If only someone had said slow down and think about it. You do really have all the time in the world. Because of social pressures it is not easy all the time but I had my whole life ahead of me. What are four years? I am convinced many people should have transferred. But if you can't transfer, it makes you work to make it work. Transferring is not that big of a deal.

Gwen senior

Transferring to a new school after freshman year was a very positive thing for me. I adapted very easily and enjoyed the new environment. I felt like I had two freshman years of meeting new people and being involved in different activities. When I transferred I immediately tried to get involved in many different social activities. This helped my adjustment and made making new friends easier. I soon discovered that transferring was not the end of the world; rather, it was a positive change with new opportunities.
Jessica

Chapter 13 Who Am I, Now?

Recently a new acquaintance asked me to tell her about me. I told her my name and what I do and then launched into a detailed description of my daughters – where they were, what they were doing, who they are. Next day I overheard a man describing every detail of his sons' lives. I realized how boring it is to listen to parents talk only about their children.

All of us enter a new phase when we send our children to college. Whether it is your first, your only or your last, life at home changes. Our lives change rhythm with the addition or subtraction of any household member; whether it is the permanent change of the arrival home from the hospital of our first child or a temporary change of an extended visit of our Florida retired parents. Today children occupy a large portion of our lives. We spend much of our time attending their sporting events, cultural performances or other activities. Often our friends are the parents of our children's friends. When our children go off to college not only is their place at the dinner table empty but the phone doesn't ring as frequently, we consider getting rid of call waiting, and our social schedules are free. If you are close enough to be able to participate there are parents' weekends and other events at the college. Your social calendar has more and more empty spaces as each child leaves. This is particularly significant for a single parent who has spent much of her time invested in her child's life. It is very important to anticipate and prepare for the change in demands on your time. The year I found both my children away at school, I renewed my interest in the local community theater and was cast in a musical, something I hadn't done since I was in high school. It is often important for us when a relationship changes or ends to rediscover some of the things that we previously enjoyed when we had only ourselves to worry about. Also this is a good time to start new interests in your life. When you are part of a couple, it's important for you to anticipate some new or forgotten old activities that you can do together. There's a wide gamut of activities out there including the possibility of traveling out of season previously precluded by the school calendar. New interests, new hobbies, new friends are critical to making this transition. Perhaps you just anticipate spending a significant amount of time thinking about what it is you want to do and trying out some new things. What is most important is anticipating that there will be a difference in the rhythm of your days, your weeks and particularly your weekends. It is to your benefit to anticipate this change and prepare for it. Remember, however, change takes time.

Frequently when your son is experiencing this transition, you too are experiencing transitions in your lives. We might be experiencing changes in our careers, a newly empty nest, the care/death of our aging parents or a change in our own health. It is important, therefore, to find other support systems to deal with our emotional angst. Our student is dealing with a particularly stressful time of growth in his life. It is important to let your son determine the frequency of contact during those early months.

Helen was homesick her first year and her parents really missed their only daughter. Her homecomings were great celebrations centered on her every need. In her junior year, however, she reported to me about her recent homecoming for a scheduled break. On her arrival home, there was a note taped to the refrigerator door, "Hi H, we are at a party, will be home later. There's food in the refrigerator. Hope you had a good trip home."

Although as recently as the year before she had lamented her parents continued over involvement in her life, this young woman was startled at the fact that her parents had moved on with their lives, and she was no longer the center of attention.

"Who am I now?" - The age-old question that both child and parent should ask of themselves. As I mentioned in the first chapter, the relationship between you and your child will go through changes. When your child was young, you were the parent. Now that your son or daughter will be taking the reigns of responsibility, you have the chance to become a friend and a parent. A balance must be struck between the two, and it might be difficult to find the happy medium. You need to let go of some control that you are used to having over your child's life. They need to show you

that they are capable of handling themselves. The smoother this process goes, the more easily you will be able to communicate as equals. You can talk to your kids about school without asking them if their homework is done.

Enjoy this opportunity to be a friend rather than a guardian. Let your child know that you will always be a parent as well, with unconditional love and support. Most importantly keep the communication open so that distance doesn't come between you and your child or your growth as individuals. Kristina

Linda L. Bips, Ed.D. with Jessica and Kristina Wallitsch

Appendix   College Services

Here are some resources for you to know about and share with your student.

Academics

Academic support – These professionals who teach study skills and learning strategies can also assess any learning problems that your son is experiencing,

Tutoring center – These paraprofessionals will tutor your daughter one-on-one in any subject. Sometimes tutors use tutors in their weak subjects while tutoring others in their strong subjects. Smart students use tutors. Frequently these students are paid by the college/university.

Writing assistance – These professionals, paraprofessionals and trained students review and critique your son's papers. They won't write the paper for your son, so he should have a draft in hand to make the best use of his time.

Faculty – All faculty post office hours for students. At a big university there may be a teaching assistant who handles the students' individual questions. Remind your daughter that communicating with her faculty is the best way to get an education.

Advising – Your son will be assigned an academic advisor who will review his course choices. When he chooses a major he may switch to a faculty member in his chosen course of study. This individual will assist your son in making course choices that lead to meeting his graduation and major requirements. Later in college, the advisor may also play a key role in assisting your son in seeking graduate admission.

Athletics

Your son may be a varsity player in a sport that practices year round, play intramurals during the fall or take a class or swim for his own personal fitness during pool hours. This office can help him meet his physical needs. This department may also provide a trainer to help your son to recover from sports related injuries.

Career services

This office is not just for seniors. Your son can receive guidance from day one about picking a major, getting a job on or off campus, or learning more about his interests and skills. Later in his college career he can use the services for resume writing, interviewing skills, alumni networking, internship placement, and even finding a job/career.

Community service

An important cure for the blues or inertia is for your daughter to volunteer to serve others. Many opportunities exist for community service from building a house to tutoring in after school programs to serving meals at a soup kitchen. Encourage your daughter to contribute to her community.

Counseling

Psychological counselors are trained professionals who counsel college students on every concern - family problems, anxiety, depression, social concerns, to name only a few. They may also provide group support for individuals who have problems with addictions, are victims of sexual assault or just experiencing every day difficulties. They also are a good resource when your daughter tells you about a friend with a problem. They also may offer educational programs in the residence hall about a variety of topics.

Deans

Deans are the Jack's and Jill's of all trades. If your daughter is not satisfied with the resolution of concerns by other professionals or just doesn't know where else to go, she should make an appointment with the Dean. Many campuses have separate deans for academic matters and for student life issues so your daughter should find out which dean is appropriate for her concern before making that appointment.

Disabilities office

Students with cognitive, physical or emotional disabilities should make their written documentation from professional evaluations available to this office. The professional staff can then advise him of appropriate accommodations such as extended test time and the procedures to obtain such accommodations.

Financial Aid

In addition to supervising your student's grants, scholarships and loans, this can be a great place to find out where the jobs on campus are. This is probably one of the first offices you will deal with during the admissions process and every year thereafter.

Health care

Doctors, nurse practitioners, nurses and health educators can be found at the campus health center. Many students start their search for help here with specific or vague complaints. Besides treating the common cold or more serious physical ailments, these professionals can refer your son to other services on campus when their complaints aren't merely physical.

Multicultural

This office provides activities and support to students from other countries and other cultures.

Residential Concerns

> **Resident Assistants** – These trained students are the first individuals to offer assistance for your daughter's roommate problems. Most colleges expect your daughter to go first to her RA with her concerns. You may meet this student on the hall on move-in day.

> **Head Residents, Building Directors, and Area Coordinators** - Professionals or para-professionals assist your daughter when the front line RA has not

been able to help the roommates resolve their differences.

Director of Residence Life/Director of Housing – On small campuses this may be the same professional with the skills and authority to resolve roommate concerns or housing problems.

Security

The campus safety officers are there to protect your daughter's safety. If she is feeling threatened or just needs an escort across campus late at night, campus safety is the office to call.

Spiritual

Depending on whether the college is private or public there may be religious organizations for your son to join. Some schools have a chaplain for different faiths. Services and counseling may be offered.

Social Life

A director of student life schedules all those wonderful entertainment activities that make a campus an exciting place to be. Frequently one or more student organizations work with this individual. This is a great office for your son to get connected to campus life.

Linda L. Bips, Ed.D. with Jessica and Kristina Wallitsch

References and Bibliography

Arnett, J.J. (2000). Emerging adulthood: A theory of development from the late teens through the twenties. *American Psychologist, 55(5),* 469-480.

Chickering, A.W. (1969). *Education and identity.* San Francisco: Jossey-Bass.

Coburn, K.L., & Treeger, M. L. (1997). *Letting go* (3rd ed.). New York: HarperCollins.

Dempster, F.N. (1988). The spacing effect: A case study in the failure to apply the results of psychological research. *American Psychologist, 43,* 627-634.

Erikson, E. (1963). *Childhood and society* (2nd ed.). New York: Norton.

Erikson, E. (1968). *Identity: Youth and crisis.* New York: Norton.

Gilligan, C. (1982). *In a different voice.* Cambridge, Mass: Harvard University Press.

Gordon, T. (1975). *Parent effectiveness training.* New York: The New American Library, Inc.

Josselson, R. (1987). *Finding herself: Pathways to identity development in women.* San Francisco: Jossey-Bass.

Kuhn C., Swartzwelder S., & Wilson, W. (1998). *Buzzed: The straight facts about the most used and abused drugs from alcohol to ecstasy.* New York: W.W. Norton & Co.

Skinner, B.F. (1953). *Science and human behavior.* New York: Macmillan

Time Magazine (April 1, 2002). Higher Education Center. Retrieved March 23, 2002 from http://www.edu.orf/hevc/pubs/binge.htm

University of California in Los Angeles (January 28, 2002). Higher Education Research Institute. Retrieved March 23, 2002, from http://www.uclanews.ucla.edu/Docs/2955.htm

About the Author

Linda Bips, psychologist, is a specialist in the transition issues of college students and their families. As the Director of Counseling and faculty at Muhlenberg College and psychologist for the Fall 2001 Semester at Sea program, she has worked with 100's of students. Personally, she has provided guidance and counsel for her two daughters, co-authors Jessica, a 1998 graduate of Muhlenberg College, and Kristina, a 2002 graduate of the University of Pennsylvania. Dr. Bips has appeared on The Oprah Winfrey Show and her work has been featured in USA Today, Seventeen, and Mademoiselle. Through her speaking, writing, teaching, and consulting, Dr. Bips has been able to help hundreds of families and students make an optimal transition to college life.

Printed in the United States
50142LVS00006B/1-120